Praise for *My Love Is a Beast: Confessions*

It's a rare memoir in which one can see themselves — a small town farm slut turned big city Queer journalist, for example — and constantly pause at the unflinching and powerful way an author recounts their own personal journey. Alexander Cheves has offered such a book in *My Love is a Beast: Confessions,* a provocative and poetic look at one young Queer man's own coming of age in rural America and through the dark days of the pandemic lockdown. As a Queer writer in America, I see myself in his exploration of the kink and fetish world, his embrace of sex work and recreational drugs, even his move from city to city in search of himself and his people. His story reflects so much of the modern Queer experience in the gay meccas of America today. Even more powerful, as Cheves moves from Atlanta to San Francisco to Los Angeles to NYC, having sex with abandon, he moves through issues including a reappraisal of what it means to be "gay" today, his role as a feminist in a male body, what is an embrace and what could be a betrayal of self. His candor around sex work and his own sexual thirsts are laid bare, very bare, in efforts to be transparent, a bit of a braggart, and to buck the stigma that comes with sex work, chemsex, and fetish play. In doing so, Cheves offers a page-turner that must leave even the hungriest of sex pigs hoping his parents never read his book. And the parents, those rural Southern Baptist kin who adopted him at birth and love him, are a feature that bookends the memoir like the duality that is contrasted throughout: love and hate, sex and death, ownership and freedom, belonging and outcast. I loved every uncomfortable minute of *My Love is a Beast: Confessions,* and it's a must-read for many folks, not just Queers. Cheves gives nods throughout, in different ways, to why you too should care, with an acknowledgement of thanks to "those who fought a plague and liberated me and all future faggots by refusing to simply die."

Diane Anderson-Minshall

CEO and Editorial Director, Pride Media and author of *Queerly Beloved: A Love Story Across Genders* and four novels.

Emerging as a much needed and influential voice, Cheves shocks while also liberating and healing readers with his vulnerable account of a journey into sexual authenticity and humanity. The honesty here sharply penetrates and stays with you long after reading. *My Love is a Beast: Confessions* cements Cheves as an important author who combines powerful storytelling with his own pain and struggles. Through its exploration of sexuality, relationships, and social trauma, this book reminds us of the beauty and bravery of living in our truth. Radical and triggering, Cheves is also brilliantly soothing.

Chris Donaghue, PhD, LCSW, CST
Host of *Loveline* and author of *Rebel Love*

Alexander Cheves encapsulates the breadth of gay male sex and identity in words so beautiful they make one weep with unbridled joy. With wisdom and insight beyond his years, Cheves has created a work of art that worships at the altar of starkly honest desire. Few writers can muster such brazen transparency. Cheves directly confronts the topic of modern gay sex with a writerly aplomb most authors never find. Savor every word of this literary bacchanal. I predict it will catapult to the top of Queer book offerings.

Race Bannon
Author and Community Leader

I read, I laughed, I cried, I jerked off — sometimes all at once. Alexander Cheves tells his story of early gay life as it should be told: terrifying, daring, angry, and so very fragile. When I first met Alexander, despite our 30-year age difference, I knew immediately I had found a comrade in the war against shame and sexual correctness. With this book, he gives me hope yet again.

Christopher Harrity
The Advocate

These revealing stories resonate profoundly. They bring a sense of relief: *finally, someone said it*. Such an act of authorial vulnerability creates life-giving intimacy. As a professional counselor, I deeply value Alexander Cheves' refusal to need a "why" regarding his kinkiness and his sexuality. This makes his work a poignant rebellion against the constant pathologizing of all things Queer. This is an important memoir in its refusal to shy away from the most taboo aspects of a young Queer man's complicated and powerful sexuality.

Amariah Love, MS, NCC, LPC

I admire Alexander Cheves for boldly and unabashedly putting to paper his thoughts and experiences around gay men's sex culture. We need more anti-assimilationist and un-sanitized Queer voices like his.

Stephan Ferris
Queer Legal Scholar and Activist Attorney

My Love Is a Beast: Confessions

My Love Is a Beast: Confessions

Alexander Cheves

UNBOUND EDITION PRESS

Atlanta

Copyright © 2021 by Alex W. Cheves
All Rights Reserved

FIRST EDITION

Printed in the United States of America

LIBRARY OF CONGRESS RECORD

Name: Cheves, Alexander, 1992– author.
Title: My Love Is a Beast : confessions / Alexander Cheves.
Edition: First edition.
Published: Atlanta : Unbound Edition Press, 2021.

LCCN: 2021937133
LCCN Permalink: https://lccn.loc.gov/2021937133
ISBN: 9780991378036 (hardcover)

Printed by Bookmobile, Minneapolis, MN
Distributed by Small Press Distribution

123456789

Unbound Edition Press
1270 Caroline Street, Suite D120
Box 448
Atlanta, GA 30307

For Dad and Mom,
who taught me to always tell the truth.

Contents

Ghosts	19	Hotel	127
Tongue	27	Backroom	135
Guide	33	Bathhouse	141
Thursday	47	Heaven	153
Eden	55	Submissive	169
Xmas	59	June	177
Airport	71	Doubles	183
Faithless	79	Atonement	195
S.F.	87	Prayer	205
L.A.	101	Virus	209
Pussy	113		

Author's Note

Some of the experiences in this book were not strictly consensual and are depicted as such. I would be lying if I denied them as being empowering and, in some cases, beautiful. But with my current knowledge and understanding, I recognize that these stories might appear to normalize, condone, and even glorify crimes like assault and rape. That is not my intention. My confessions should be viewed only as what they are: a personal effort to weave my own life into meaning.

Publisher's Disclaimer

This book is a memoir. It reflects the author's present recollections of events, experiences, and conversations over time. In order to maintain anonymity and privacy, some names and characteristics have been changed, some events have been compressed, and some dialogue has been recreated. The views expressed are solely the author's, and do not reflect the official policy or position of Unbound Edition, LLC.

My Love Is a Beast: Confessions

Inside these breast-bones I lie smutch'd and choked;
Beneath this face that appears so impassive, hell's tides continually run;
Lusts and wickedness are acceptable to me;
I walk with delinquents with passionate love;
I feel I am of them — I belong to those convicts and prostitutes myself,
And henceforth I will not deny them — for how can I deny myself?

Walt Whitman
from "You Felons on Trial in Courts"

Words without experience are meaningless.

Vladimir Nabokov
from *Lolita*

Ugh, I'm so sick & tired of that woman's orifices!

Don Moss
regarding Sharon Olds

Ghosts

My father was walking through the woods when he heard something strange. He had been forming these trails since he was a boy, running around unsupervised on his grandfather's land. He kicked away the leaves and muck on the path. What he found was no lost dog or injured coyote. It was smaller, hidden near the roots of a shagbark hickory tree. He carried it back to the house, bringing me into his world.

Adopted children often invent their own creation myths. I knew I was not from my parents, but I was theirs. I did not ask the inevitable questions until I was almost a teenager, after I learned that the beginning of a person is sex and pain. *Fucking*.

They knew nothing about the woman who birthed me except that she was described in the adoption papers as *a dancer*, a 1992 code word for *prostitute*, or so I've always believed. At first, I envisioned her as a ballerina or Broadway starlet, someone doing a bawdy number in a sequined dress. But this seems unlikely.

I grew up on a river, an early branch of the Ogeechee, which runs through my family's land. My childhood was colored by its sandbanks, its smell, and its chill. As a child, I was skinny and loud, big-lipped, pouty. I played on the rocks of the river, got wet, ruined my clothes. My parents thought something was wrong with me because, when they called me, I ignored them and kept running — onto the train tracks, into traffic, across the river stones. When I was four, they learned the reason: I was deaf in my right ear and simply didn't hear them. They adjusted — learned which side to talk to — and discovered, as I did, that in addition to my reduced hearing, I was simply disobedient.

I was not very athletic, but I grew up alongside kids who hunted and fished, and although I was not much like them, I understood them.

In my last year of college, I felt a strange pull, something like homesickness, but not for the place I was supposed to call home. I belonged to the woods and river, but I did not belong to the house, where so many family fights had hurt everyone involved.

In that final, restless year of school, I missed something about the river and the rural men I used to love. I was planning to leave the Deep South for good and never come back. And because of my coming exodus, I already missed the hunters in camouflage who came to shoot deer in the woods when I was younger. I missed the guys from my varsity football team who spit chewing tobacco into plastic cups in their mud-splattered pickup trucks. I missed farm boys, guys who smelled like earth. So, I started driving outside Savannah, my college town, on weekends to meet guys in the country.

We fucked in barns, in the backs of trailers, on the beds of work trucks. We fucked in the woods. These men smelled familiar, like oil. I imagined them all having just crawled out from under a car at an auto shop.

My favorite playmates were two guys, a couple, who lived an hour outside of town. Their house was at the end of a long dirt road, far from the main highway. When I drove up to their place for the first time, I saw a chicken coop and two old pickups in the yard. They cooked me dinner, showed me the chickens and the garden out back, and after dark, took me to the bedroom.

+ + +

I kissed the taller man as he pulled me onto the bed. Together, the two pulled off my pants with a coordinated and practiced tug.

"Wait," I said. "I haven't cleaned out."

"We don't care."

The taller man unbuckled his belt, a big silver cowboy buckle, and slid down his pants and underwear. His dick flopped out and it was the biggest one I'd seen at that point.

Go ahead, suck it.

I could barely fit it in my mouth. But with a focused pressure and thrust, a wrist-thick part of someone else was packed into my airway. He cupped the back of my head and pushed me down on it. When I gagged, I felt like I had failed, but he seemed proud of me.

He pulled me to his face and kissed me. I smelled beer. He had a salt-and-pepper beard. His partner was watching us. "Sit on it," he instructed and produced a bottle of K-Y water-based lube from the bedside table — the cheap stuff that teenagers buy at gas stations. I rubbed his dick with the goo and tried to mount it, but it delivered a jolt of pain, so I pulled off.

The other man, the one watching, came up behind me and started massaging my shoulders. "You're so tense," he said. "You gotta relax if you're gonna take that."

"Yeah, it's a nice dick." I didn't think I could do it.

"Try again," the man below me said. "Just breathe." He fingered my butthole as I straddled his belly, and I could tell his fingers were calloused, his palms rope-burnt, fingernails untrimmed. The guy behind me was gentler and softer, and I guessed he was usually the bottom. He wanted to see my hole resized by his reliable aggressor.

I tried again, slowly.

The man seemed annoyed that I was struggling with it. He put both hands around my hips and pushed me down. I yelped like a kicked dog.

I don't remember everything about that night, but I remember the yelp, the beautiful sound of being taken by force. The man behind me rubbed my shoulders; the man below kissed my neck.

"It's so thick." I whimpered.

This might really hurt me.

"I know, baby boy. I got you."

He's got me.

His boyfriend whispered in my ear: "You can do it." The man behind me had a stronger accent, more honeyed, longer vowels, and I guessed he was from South Georgia. The man I was riding was less discernable — North Carolina, maybe.

"You got it," South Georgia said. "You're halfway there." I heard him spit heavily, then felt his dick pushing in over the one in me.

I sat up. "I can't do that."

No, no. I haven't ...

"Yes, you can," North Carolina said.

South Georgia held a cold bottle of poppers — an inhalant people like me use to relax sphincter muscles and take dick up the butt — beneath my nose and told me to breathe in deeply. I was new to poppers and did too much. In a moment, my vision blurred, and I started a euphoric spinning, my hole opening.

The men rubbed me the way I needed to be rubbed, the way I wanted guys from high school to rub me. They had that earthy tractor smell, and I melted in their words, became liquid metal, invincible. South Georgia slid his dick in, and it felt like I was being split.

This is some dark heaven, some raging joy.

They pushed on my shoulders more firmly, holding me down to keep me from pushing off of them.

I took the pain.

I can take the pain. Anything for cock like this.

They kissed me, kissed my neck, and then they were moving together inside me. I could feel both of them, sliding in cadence, in and out, and I drowned in it. They later said that they did this all the time with bottoms who came over. They had perfected it.

It's perfect. Perfect.

I don't remember the end of that night, just their rhythm, how stretched and powerful I felt. I don't remember if anyone came or if I swallowed their cum or if I was bred by them.

After sex, we got stoned and went to the shower, where they bathed me in kindness. I was between two older brothers, witnesses to my transfiguration.

I am a hole now.

Their soap was almond-scented, and we smelled sweet all night. The rugged top with the massive cock fell asleep first and the gentler man stayed up with me drinking a beer. He asked about my tattoos.

"You got words on yer rib cage," he said.

"It's the penultimate stanza of a poem called 'Heaven' by Jack Kerouac." I was proud of my knowledge, carnal and poetic.

"Who's that?"

"A writer. My favorite."

"What's it say?"

And the little mouse
that I killed will devour

me into its golden belly.
That little mouse was God.

"That don't make much sense to me," he said, "but you're beautiful."

+ + +

Driving back to Savannah the next morning, I was sore and there actually was a little bit of blood. But I felt electrified, reborn. I avoided the highway and took a longer way back, through dead towns with a single traffic light, brick buildings with weeds in the sidewalk. I drove past yellowing pickup trucks abandoned in yards, gas stations where people sat outside in plastic chairs, houses falling in. The town near my family's farm was one like these.

I have to go.

I thought about the men, their bodies moving together, mine between them. They did not go to the gym, but they were strong as horses. Their bodies were made to push wheelbarrows and lift bales of hay. Their sex was unrefined, unsullied by porn or ass douching or the glittery details of urban gay life. It was the rough, exploratory sex I learned while still in the closet. Their Southern world, the one I wanted to leave, looked mysterious and beautiful to me as if I saw it for the first time.

This could have been home.

I got back to my dorm room and fell asleep. I had a haunting dream. It was in black and white, an old movie already running somewhere in my mind. No other dream had been like this.

+ + +

I am walking along a beach. At the edge of the beach, there's a black forest. I walk through fir trees and see a fire in a clearing ahead. The fire flickers through the branches, electric white.

It is night. I hear laughing and the clinking of bottles, and when I step through the branches, I see William Burroughs sitting on a stump. Jack Kerouac is waving a half-empty bottle over his head. Allen Ginsberg plays a flute. Neal Cassady whoops and hollers, "He's here! He's here!"

T. S. Eliot walks through the bushes, his black hair parted in the middle. Vladimir Nabokov appears, small white moths clinging to the shoulders of his tatty coat. Shel Silverstein says hello. There are others I don't know, all writers, all dead. Ginsberg howls at the moon.

We start running through the woods. I see more of them coming in across the field, their lanterns flickering in the dark. Someone shouts: "Over here!" I realize we're all ghosts.

Then we are on the beach. Kerouac runs up behind me and jumps on my back. His stubble scratches my ear and I smell liquor on his breath. I put my arms under his legs and carry him into the surf. The black ocean feels open, limitless, icy. Others push behind me and I ask: "Are y'all coming?"

+ + +

Are y'all coming? Please come.

Y'all, please come.

I had worked for years to shed my Southern accent, the dumb of my words, promising myself to never say *y'all*. But no more. Now I had found home, among the woods and men, writers and ghosts. And my native tongue flicked alive in my mouth, as if for the first time.

Tongue

Billy Habersham was a ridiculous person, but what we did could have happened with any other hole. For some weeks during my freshman year of college, we were boyfriends.

Boyfriends.

The word tasted like fire. When I said it, I felt like I was committing a crime in broad daylight. What would my parents think?

I hear them mumblin', I hear the cacklin'
I got 'em scared, shook, panickin'
Overseas, church, Vatican
You at a standstill, mannequin

One night, Billy was knocking on every door in our dormitory, going from room to room saying hello, dipping and bowing his head, laughing at everything. His teasing sense of humor had teeth in it, which I believed was an overcompensation. He was very short with a high, throaty voice, blonde hair, and wicked, darting green eyes.

I don't know how he came to be standing in my room, but once there, he announced his name and explained that his brown leather jacket was custom fitted in the leather markets of Florence, Italy, where he visited during his last year of high school. I don't know why he told this story, but it seemed to be his version of an introduction. He was a sprite in pressed pants, loafers, and a silly knitted hat that was only big enough for him to wear on one side of his head, over one ear. With his height, the hat made him look like some Disney cartoon character.

I am not Jasmine, I am Aladdin
So far ahead, these bums is laggin'
See me in that new thing, bums is gaggin'
I'm startin' to feel like a dungeon dragon

Enraptured by his Southern, genteel nature, I fell in love with him. Even at his shorter height, his body bristled with strength, and when he got drunk, he became hard to handle. He screamed and sang through the streets of Savannah in the early hours some mornings, and when I tried to grab him to take him back to the dorms, he easily pushed me away and ran off giggling.

One night he stopped resisting, relented, pushed me against a tree. We kissed drunkenly, feverishly, and I said we should go back and take a shower. When we arrived at my room, he was shout-rapping a popular song, "Roman's Revenge" by Nicki Minaj featuring Eminem. He continued doing this in the bathroom as I took off his clothes. My roommates were trying to sleep on the other side of the wall.

When we were wet, I told him I wanted to eat his ass. He asked if I'd ever done it before.

"No. Have you?"

Never. I'm kind of scared.

"No."

I got on my knees and started kissing his legs, building myself up to do this thing. He was standing under the water and finally I said, "Billy, I'm drowning. Can we switch places?" He was so blisteringly drunk that it was hard to make him move to the other side of the shower, and he was still shout-singing, the shower making his voice echo even louder.

He had the most perfect ass, pale and round, with soft blonde hairs running up his crack, and when I pulled it apart with my hands, I saw his hole, eye-to-eye. It was baby pink, a tight screw of skin, like the knot of a balloon, begging to be pried open. I tried picturing us from above, wet and new like creatures in Eden, one man standing, pushing his butt out, the other kneeling behind him, gazing, studying.

In wonder.

The water ran in little rivulets around his pucker. I took a breath, placed my tongue on it, and licked as if I was licking for the first time, discovering the motion meant for my tongue.

I braced myself for some horrible taste, because this was where he ...

It's poop, Alex.

But mostly I just tasted sweat, and if there was anything else, it tasted sweet. His hole was so beautiful and tight that I could hardly slide my tongue in it. I didn't know how this was done or what I was supposed to do to be good at it. Billy finally stopped rapping and groaned, resting his head in his arm in the corner of the shower.

I was afraid of buttholes before that night. The animal in me feared bad smells. They are nature's signs of rot and toxicity, things that could kill my ancestors if eaten. So, my hesitancy in the shower was just a primitive fear of eating what could harm me. But that night was the first time I was unafraid of sticking my tongue into danger, working against my evolution to become a full-on faggot. Rimming him was both risk and reward in the same moment, and I licked his pink bud, barely opening for me, like it was soft butter.

Raah, raah, like a dungeon dragon
I'm startin' to feel like a dungeon dragon

+ + +

Billy was Methodist and insisted we go to church. I told him I would never set foot in a church again. Though he never admitted this to me, I think my disdain for his beliefs — not the drinking and the childish mistakes that came with it — made our relationship so brief.

But sometime in the brief weeks while we were dating, he convinced me to attend a service at the Unitarian Universalist Church of Savannah, which claimed to welcome everyone, even someone like me. Instead of hymns or worship songs, we sang "Imagine" by John Lennon. The sermon was about community love, humility — a hybrid of liberal Christianity mixed with a generic egalitarian humanism that viewed people as the most beloved creation. While the church was a nice departure from the Southern Baptists I grew up with, I did not believe that humans were that special.

"Fine, you don't have to go next time," he said.

In the garden outside the church, we fought. I started mocking him. I told him I didn't want to worship a paltry god of flawed people. He walked away pissed.

The world, world is my punchin' bag and
If I am garbage, you're a bunch of maggots
Make that face, go on, scrunch it up at me
Show me the target so I can lunge and attack it

Our breakup was messy (beach, alcohol, older boys, cheating, drama). A week later, I walked toward the dorm, drunk, and started crying. I was overwrought in my young gay hysteria, and nearly collapsed in the street, dry heaving, sobbing. Friends had to pull me up and convince me to keep walking. That breakup felt so serious and heavy. It was my first, and I really believed I would never love again.

Billy Habersham welcomed me into the rich brutality of heartbreak and gave me my first taste of ass, too. We didn't speak for years after. Later, we reconnected as grown men, crawled into bed again, and forgave. I wondered if he had been as changed by it all as much as I had.

Raah, raah, like a dungeon dragon
Like a dungeon dragon, like a dungeon dragon

Guide

Professor Arnold was in her forties with golden hair that fell just past her shoulders. She printed copies of poems from the Internet and handed them out at the start of every class before selecting someone to read aloud. When the chosen classmate finished butchering Elizabeth Bishop or Li-Young Lee, the professor re-read the poem, and it was breathtaking every time. She had no sense of embarrassment or shame and read with every emotion available to her. She read with her body and soul.

"Listen up," she said. "You have to learn to read your work to yourself and others. It's okay to feel stupid. Sometimes poetry is stupid."

One day I turned in a poem about Disney World and she said, "This makes me angry, Alex, because I know you're better than this. And there is nothing more horrible, more *grotesque*, than Disney World."

It's a small world, after all.

When I cheated on my boyfriend and gave him chlamydia, I turned in a poem about how everyone does horrible things in order to grow.

"I bet that makes you feel a lot better about yourself," she said.

After class, as I was packing up my things, she told me to wait. "Alex, I'm surprised to hear that you're not a good boyfriend." I didn't know what to say. She looked at me sadly. "You know you can't just go around hurting people and thinking it means nothing."

Her own stories became so real in my mind that I felt I was there, in her life, even though I wasn't. I wasn't in her kitchen when her three-year-old daughter was talking about Timmy, the neighbor's son who was mean, and said, "I just wish he could understand me." The professor gasped and realized: we are never fully understood by anyone.

I wasn't with her in the supermarket when she was talking on the phone with her husband (a professor who taught a class on the Beat Poets called "Angelheaded Hipsters") and told him she didn't want to be alone at the house that night. Her three-year-old daughter, riding in the little seat of the cart, grabbed her chin and said, "Mommy, you'll never be alone." That had haunted her ever since.

I wasn't with her when she walked out of the building after a real shit day and a homeless person walked by and shouted "Everythin' gon' be alright!" and she burst into tears.

Her stories served no practical purpose but to teach and confound her students, and they burrowed into me, and have never left. Years later, I spoke to classmates who took those courses with me and we all remembered her stories more than any single lesson or poem.

None of us could understand poetry because we were trying to understand it. We thought there was something to grasp, a secret to unlock.

"The worst thing you can do is drag a poem into the middle of the room and beat a meaning out of it," she said passionately when we did not understand. She was my literary mother.

She gave me Sharon Olds, Billy Collins, Allen Ginsberg, C. K. Williams, William Carlos Williams, Mary Oliver, Matthew Dickman, and Mark Strand. Where would I be without these? "But," she said one day, standing at the front of the classroom: "There are poems I will never give you, because they mean too much to me and I have to keep them to myself. And you have to find your own poems like that."

She gave me all these things and I never said thanks. I lost touch with her. My poetry was published a few times in the little literary magazine on campus, which she edited and compiled, and I think she cared for me deeply. But when I was gone, I was gone.

She would think me ridiculous for writing a book about my sex life and work. She would probably tell me that I'm likely to face the same sort of criticism thrown at Sharon Olds, her favorite poet, who male critics have generally blasted for always writing about her sex and her body. "It must be very gratifying," Professor Arnold would say. Or possibly, "Alex, this is one giant booty call."

Yes, ma'am.

She would laugh and walk away. That would be her approval.

+ + +

Poetry was my original language of sex. I understood orgasm editorially — the same way I understood dying and growing old — but I couldn't express the fear, desire, or anguish of these experiences without roping in the language of prayer.

Oh, metaphor.

Describing the body, I generally attempted comparisons. Orgasm as flying. Pleasure as honey and water. Sex as pink and skin, bursting and spilling.

Let us now kneel.

I once turned in a poem about growing up on my parents' farm and the time I stepped over a small black snake in the field and ran away screaming. "Alex, it's just a little black snake!" Dad said. "It's not a cottonmouth. You have to be able to tell the difference."

I was proud of the poem, but when I read it to the class, everyone commented that they didn't get the "Black cock" reference. I said it wasn't a Black cock reference. And everyone said it had to be.

Oh, metaphor. I kneel.

"Alex, I sympathize," Professor Arnold said. "I believe you really saw the snake and are talking about an actual snake. I wrote a poem in college about an encounter with a snake and everyone said the same thing. And I'm sorry to say this, but you can't divorce the two. If you write about a snake, it's a dick. It's always going to be a dick."

"So how do I write about a dick?"

Write what you know.

"It's hard to write about sex directly without comparing it to animals or objects. There are just some things you can't get away with in poetry anymore. You can't get away with someone crying or tears, because it's just too cheap. And blood is such a strong image that it overpowers a poem. The second you write *blood*, all we see is blood. And penises and sex when written about literally can throw a poem. The best poetry about sex uses fruit and meat and household objects and turns them into the terrain of the body."

Then she stopped for a moment and looked down. Everyone held their breath.

"That said, most people are just writing about sex. Or death. Or fear of sex. Or fear of death. Sex is difficult to write about because it's ubiquitous. Sex and death are in everything, they are the beginning and the end."

I am the Alpha and the Omega.

+ + +

She told us stories about her engagement with the world — about the girl selling kittens near the supermarket. The kittens were still blind, too young to be away from their mother.

"And I had to tell her this," the professor said. "But she didn't understand me, so I told her in Spanish that these kittens were too young, and many of them will die."

Someone asked if she was fluent in Spanish and the professor said, "Of course."

Why?

"I wanted to read Pablo Neruda in the language he's supposed to be read in."

She told us stories about travel. I don't think there were any textbook lessons. I just read poems — mine, those of my classmates, and the ones Professor Arnold gave us — and talked about them. Grades came largely from discussions, from the willingness to talk about things personal and important. There was no way to fail her classes, except not to care. I cared, but more than that, I wanted to be a good poet, and I wanted her to recognize in me some kind of prophet.

What a bold boy.

Instead, she saw me as I was, a privileged kid who took to rebellion because it was fun, a boy who liked to bullshit people for reaction. I was writing poetry with cruelty and anger, mostly about my parents, and one day she said, "Alex, has it ever occurred to you that you're in this class because of them?"

I am a cliché, a rebel choking on a silver spoon.

I told her — again, after class — that she was the kind of parent I wish I had, because she would never shame her three-year-old daughter for being gay. Professor Arnold was worldly and progressive and liberal. She spoke about sex and desire like they were natural, good things.

"But does that mean I will never fail?" she asked, upset with me. I wondered if I had crossed a line. "Every parent fails a little bit." Then she told me about a moment she had with her father. They were in a garden or riding horseback, something like that, and at that moment, she realized she was his equal — she was no longer a daughter and had to decide if she was his friend. And she realized there was nothing to hate about him, nothing more to ask of him. And she said that when I came to that moment in the garden, I'd have to make a choice, too.

"Travel is so important," she told the class one day. We'd already agreed that music was important, and sex was important. What else?

"You only recognize the world you're in by leaving it and being confronted with people who live differently than you do. You have to travel as much as you can, and you have to do it now. Don't wait until you're retired or something stupid like that. There's no saving you at that point."

Spurred on by W. S. Merwin, I wrote a poem about leaving — leaving my lovers, my family, my life behind — and going to Africa, guided by indigenous spirits. I wrote the poem because I had lived in Zambia, Africa for a few years when I was little, while my parents, both of them doctors, operated at a hospital funded by the Southern Baptist Convention. I missed Africa, its clear stars and its smells, a bouquet of grass and dust. I called the poem "The Guide."

The professor read it and put it down. "You've written about what everyone wants," she said. "Someone to hold our hands. Someone to show us the way. It is a prayer. But you don't need W. S. Merwin, Alex. It's a good start, but you have to start walking on your own two feet."

+ + +

One day a student in the writing department was riding her bike and got hit by a car in front of our building and was smeared across the sidewalk. She was in Professor Arnold's other poetry class. The girl survived but was put in intensive care, and the doctors said she would likely suffer cognitively and might not walk again. Professor Arnold visited her in the hospital at least once a week.

One day the professor came into class furious. "Okay, everyone. I stood outside and watched you lock up your bikes, and no one was wearing a *goddamn* helmet. If I see you riding your bike and I don't see a helmet by your desk in this class, I'll mark you absent." Four absences meant automatic failure of the class.

She told us updates about the girl. One day she stood at the front of the class and in the middle of the lesson, she started crying. We feared the worst.

"They asked her to write her mother's name on a piece of paper," she said. "Her mother's name is Sharon, so she wrote Sharon. And then they asked her to write her mother's last name, and she wrote *Olds*."

Sharon Olds.

I looked around the room. Others were crying too. I wanted to cry, but I've never been able to cry in front of people like that.

"You're all trying so hard," she said. "I get it. But you're just kids. You don't have to put yourselves under so much pressure all the time."

At that moment, we were understood. How did she know? Everyone told us to make good grades, excel, try harder. In America, we were never just kids. We came of age with cyber predators and social media, new threats, new compromises.

The girl did not die but she did not return to school. I never found out what happened to her. I bought a helmet.

One day a girl in my class turned in a poem about a pumpkin. She had just been dumped by her boyfriend of several years, and the poem was about a pumpkin that got carved out, painted, turned into a jack-o'-lantern, and made to sit there and look pretty, only to get thrown away after Halloween. The parallel was obvious. Her breakup was messy, and we all knew what was going on.

After the girl read her poem aloud, she burst into tears. "I thought the poem was really funny, but now I realize it's not funny. I think ... *I'M THE PUMPKIN!*" And she sobbed in her chair.

Oh, metaphor.

Everyone looked at the floor, mortified for her.

Professor Arnold leaned back on her desk, crossed her arms, and said, "I'm sorry to tell you this, but no one thought that poem was funny."

She let the girl cry for several minutes, then said, "Stop crying and listen up."

The girl stopped crying.

"You think you hate him, but you don't," the professor said. She took a step into the middle of the room. "You think no one else will make you feel this way, no one else will have the power to do this to you. But they will, again and again. And this is right. This is what you're *supposed* to be doing at this age. Getting your heart broken. And you tell yourself you're not that mean, that you'll never do something like this to anyone else. And you will."

No one spoke.

"Right, Alex?" She looked at me. But it was not menacing, there was a wink in there. She knew I could take it, because she knew I was not cruel.

I hope I am not cruel.

For much of my life, I was an insecure boy covered in acne. By the time I reached college, the acne was gone, and I discovered that I liked cheating, because it meant I was wanted by more than one person at a time. Deceit gave me power, but Professor Arnold taught me not to grow up into that person.

I hope I am not cruel.

My first attempt at sex writing — though I did not know that's what it was — came in the last poem I submitted to the little literary magazine. Professor Arnold asked me to read it at an awards ceremony, where she introduced me to the dean of the writing department, who was a short, bald man with round glasses and a colorful bowtie. He seemed to me like a popcorn vendor at a county fair. I was terrified of meeting him and he was far more chipper than I had imagined him to be. I pictured this god of writing as a dark creature kneeling over our building, steam coming from its nostrils, watching us. This man was nothing like that. He told me my poem was *smart* and then left.

The poem was about a dance. I had a crush on a girl at a local coffee shop, and I imagined we went dancing at one of the bars downtown. She was much smaller, and I wrote that her bones fit inside my bones and we were able to dance as one person.

Professor Arnold put the poem down and said, "You did it."

+ + +

The Love Song of an All-American Hero

This is not a dance.
This is a swarm of bodies,
black lights, mascara,
v-necks and bowties.

I want to kick a football poem
through the field goal
and make literature
sexy again.

I've changed into a shirt with a wolf on it
because I have returned to nature.

Everyone is dressed like they never cared
about anything but this night, maybe.

The girl with a brown neck like an oiled
salad fork comes up and yells
do you want to dance
and I yell back
yes.

I don't tell her I'm gay or that I can't dance
sober. I touch her
lower back. She is so small

I could fit her bones inside
my bones and we could dance
as one person.

She grinds her ass
against me
and I sniff her neck
like Walt Whitman sniffing bananas
at the supermarket
in California.

Maybe someone is jealous of me.
I would be too. She is beautiful and
she faces me, pulls my hands
to her rib cage and I let her
because I am terrified of
loneliness
and for hours
like a horse
I beat hooves against a glittering
cement floor.

Forget the love song and the Moderns and the sinking
ship and cartoon princesses wishing on computer-animated
stars. No one is coming for us.

I want to be a Western man reading the paper,
marginalized, a demographic, well-dressed,

angry at oppression in a globalized
marketplace of ideas.

I want to say love is dead,
drink coffee black
and wake up one day to find I cannot
take it anymore,
board a plane to India,
or travel the road to experience
Dharma, self-actualization,
1950s jazz
and a reclaiming
of ethnocentric, heavy-hearted
America.

But what I want most
is to take your body
in the dark and fold it

at the knees, to wade into the
primordial watering hole
and dip you.

Everyone leans together
headpiece filled with straw
when the electric music
drops.

Your ankles are broken.
You are moving in me. Strangers
are everywhere. Some guy
shoulder to shoulder to me
smells amazing.

I carry you, brown neck,
water through your arms,
there are no human voices here.

I want to hold somebody under.
My mouth meets your mouth.
I want to hear nothing
but the muted body without skin,
the electric cable of the night,
all the books on their shelves.

A collection of muscles.
The robin on the Stop sign,
The champagne glass on the table,
the leather and amber
landscape painting,

the dragon against the dumpster
filled with red corsages.

Thursday

The time was about nine in the morning and my first class was at 11. This was the moment when the frames slowed down, when each detail glitched.

I am slow motion.

Old, uneven hexagonal stones of the sidewalk. Black iron gate around the building. I walked into the small waiting room. When I told them my name, they led me down a hallway into another little room. One wall was exposed brick and there was a large potted plant in the corner. A girl was sitting in there and I asked her what she was waiting for.

"Just a routine checkup."

I took that as a good sign.

Okay. Okay. Where's the bathroom.

When the doctor walked in — a stern-faced woman with shoulder-length blond hair — she looked at the girl and said, "Are you with *him*?" The girl looked at me and shook her head. "Okay," the doctor said tersely, "I need you to leave."

"Where should I — "

"Go to the main waiting room. You can't be in here."

The doctor closed the door. That's when I knew what it was.

No. No, no. I can't.

I was actually having a panic attack, though I did not know it. I was crouching in the corner of the room on the floor next to the potted plant, rocking on my knees as the doctor sat down on the sofa. I didn't give her a chance to speak.

"Is it HIV?"

It's HIV.

She sucked her teeth. "Yeah."

It's HIV.

An hour or so later, whenever I was calm enough to talk about the next steps, I asked her how many students had tested positive that year. I was the second in six months.

"All gay?"

I am cursed. This is my fault.

"Since I've been here, yes."

She averted her eyes. She was embarrassed for me.

I don't remember the conversation we had or the nurses who came in and out of the room, but one of them was a therapist. They feared I was going to kill myself, and I knew I had to say something hopeful so they would let me leave. I asked the doctor if she had other duties and she said, "You are what I'm doing today." She wore a necklace with a tiny gold cross on it, and I asked her about it, which prompted a conversation about her church. "What about you?" she asked.

"I'm not religious."

I'm dirty.

"That's too bad. God could help."

"He could, in theory, yes."

She wrote down the name of a Christian youth group at a local church and said, "Don't worry, they're very accepting," meaning they would welcome an HIV-positive faggot. She looked at me like a distressed mom and didn't try to hide her sadness or disappointment, her deep frown. Later, I dropped off a thank-you note for her at the front desk, but after that day I never saw her again.

When I walked out of the clinic, it was early evening. The shadows from the canopy of oak trees along the street were just beginning to stretch along the sidewalk. Someone from the clinic had called my professors and told them I had a medical emergency and could not attend classes that day, which I thought was very kind.

I knew only one person with HIV, a gay man who I had rejected a few weeks earlier when he told me he was positive. And I didn't just reject him — I got angry, yelled, left his apartment, drove away. At some point in the blurred hours at the clinic, I called him, and because he was a saint, he stopped what he was doing and drove there, sat in the little room with me, and produced a pill from his shirt pocket. "This is it," he said. "This is HIV. Nothing to be afraid of."

I've lost touch with him, but if I could talk to him now, I would tell him what I've learned: that he should not have come, that the kid who refused to touch him did not deserve his kindness. I would tell him, as I have told others, that those who reject must be abandoned. They cannot be saved, helped, or forgiven.

I cannot undo what I have done.

+ + +

When I was six years old, my family moved to Zambia. My parents were medical missionaries and moved there to work at a hospital funded by a Christian organization in the United States. Everyone who came to the hospital had AIDS and everyone died. I saw their bodies in the hallways, their scars and dried lips, flies crawling across their faces. Once, Dad brought me to a little hut in a bush village. When he opened the door, I was not certain that the people we saw in there were alive. They were all black skin wrapped around bone, leaning together. They looked at us and did not speak. "They have AIDS," he said.

+ + +

I went to classes that following week, but internally I was elsewhere. I planned to kill myself that Thursday. Thursdays have always been my favorite day of the week, so it seemed a good day to go. My decision was not because of AIDS or even my imagined future, my body rotting off the bone. I chose death because my diagnosis was proof that everything Dad had told me about gay people — everything he warned me about this life — was coming true. He was right.

I came out when I was sixteen. But that's not really true, because "coming out" implies a decision, a choice. Dad confronted me in my bedroom one night, and somewhere in those horrible hours, he said, "You'll die of AIDS before you're thirty." Here I was, beating his prediction by almost a decade. How embarrassing.

+ + +

In the two months after my diagnosis, I found other ways to cope instead of dying. One night, I chatted with a guy online. He met me on Savannah's historic River Street and took me to dinner. He was nice.

After we ate, we walked to his pickup truck, parked in a remote lot near the water, and he started kissing me. I said nothing about my HIV status — honestly, I didn't know how. He pulled me into his truck, pushed the passenger seat back, took down my pants, and told me to sit on his dick.

I rode it like a god, looking down at him, nearly snarling. I shook the truck, kicked the dashboard, and spat on his face. I watched him come inside me, his face splintering in the dark, his mouth open. He looked up at me in reverie, my body crouching over him like the demon in Fuseli's *The Nightmare*. As I walked away from his truck, leaving him gasping and the windows fogged, I blocked his number.

That was how it started. Sex can be a lifeline, even when it's cruel. I later learned that manic sex periods are not especially uncommon reactions to an HIV diagnosis. I was highly infectious during this time because I was not yet on medication.

I'm supposed to explain all this and say it was *done in madness or sorrow*, or perhaps say that *I didn't know what I was doing*. But I knew what I was doing. I don't know why I did it all except that I believed I was dying soon and needed whatever it gave me. I had to feel something, and this was it.

I mostly just got fucked, and because of the mechanics of anal sex, it's much harder to transmit HIV as a bottom. But it's not impossible, and I still don't know if I infected anyone during that time. On my saddest days, I had multiple anonymous hookups a day, running from class to hotel room to strangers' cars in the middle of the night. I was heartbroken.

Walking through the neighborhoods near my dorm late at night on my way to a fuck with someone I would never see again, I felt something strange: the first taste of power through sex. I felt monstrous, and that was better, at the moment, than caving in.

You have no idea what I am.

The first person to touch me knowing I had HIV was a drag queen. We were both masquerading on the edges of gay life. I don't know why I decided to tell him the truth of my status — I had lied to many guys by that point — but he was kind and seemed like a good person. When I told him, it came out like an apology, a blight I hoped he would overlook.

After I said it, he was quiet for a few moments, then kissed me. I started crying. I did not believe anyone would ever take me with a virus.

+ + +

For three years of college, I planned to go to graduate school and get my Ph.D. to teach literature. But after HIV, I decided against that. I needed to be gay, whatever that meant. I knew nothing. A culture was out there, and I needed to chase it.

I started meds and took my pills as prescribed. And I started telling potential playmates about my HIV. Guys my age — college students — knew nothing about HIV and turned me down every time, so my sex partners shifted to older men who needed less education and were less afraid. I met another HIV-positive man named Santiago, a passionate, hung Cuban in his thirties who lived just down the street.

Santiago had a jet-black beard and beautiful cock. The first time we fucked, I felt so guilty and ashamed after my manic sex period that I said we couldn't have sex without a condom.

"Papi," he said, "We're positive. I want to fuck you, and you want me to fuck you. And you want me to fuck you bare."

I said *okay*.

His dick was heavy, uncut. He slapped my face with it and told me to kiss the tip, and when he pulled it away, a bead of pre-cum from the folds of his foreskin made a little string, like a spider web, from my lip. I remember thinking there was poison in it — the same poison in me. It was so fat that I told him I couldn't take it.

I can. I do.

"You *can*, papi," he said, holding me down. He held my wrists. "It's not too big. You can take it." I took it.

He was the first official fuck buddy of my new life. One night, he took me to a Chinese restaurant, and while we were eating, a guy I was messaging on an app blocked me. I had just told him about my status. This had happened so many times that I had grown accustomed to rejection, but something about that one left me quiet, stunned. I couldn't eat.

"What's wrong, papi?"

I told him what happened.

He told me to look at him because this was important. "Papi, it's something in your blood. That's it. You got something in your blood. If that's all that someone sees, fuck them! They don't fucking deserve you."

For many months of that year, I had little to live on, so I lived for his cum. I could mount my life on that. When I held his shoulders and felt him trembling, unloading into me, I forgot about this disease. Nothing in us was wrong. We were not ugly.

I am transformed yet again.

HIV and AIDS, in their various narratives, have been construed as everything from justice to cruelty to god's angry judgment. But it's none of those things. When I was with him, HIV was just what he said it was: something in our blood that meant nothing.

Meaningless, incarnate.

"You love bareback" Santiago spat. "You're such a pig. You *love* it."
I loved it. I lived to get bred.

One day, he had the idea to bring an inflatable mattress to the beach and sleep under the stars. We made it till four in the morning when we were freezing and decided to go home. But for a few hours, the ocean was calm, and I was warm beside him.

"Papi, go to sleep," he breathed in my ear as he held me, "Or do you want me to put it in you?"

"No," I said. "I just want to be here."

"Okay, papi."

I made it to Thursday. I made it past Thursday.

Eden

In Africa, when I was six, I wanted to climb every tree, even forbidden ones. I climbed the massive fig tree in our front yard and all the rough, scratchy ones with footlong gourds and oversized seed pods. Trees were dangerous in Africa. My parents warned me about green mambas, one of the most poisonous snakes in the world, which like to hang out in trees where their bright skin blends into the leaves.

I never encountered a snake, but with no concept of death, I thought the idea was thrilling.

It's a dick. It's always going to be a dick.

We lived in a small village in Zambia. My father visited the country first on a missionary trip, then brought my mother, and then they decided to bring me and my sister along for a few years. The entire experience of living there was marked by an isolated, religious fervency, a sense that we were suffering in an impoverished country to bless the Zambians with knowledge of Christ. While I don't think my parents were as out-of-touch as some white missionaries or wholly oblivious to the problematic "white savior" concept, Dad was nevertheless threatened by the native spiritualisms.

At Victoria Falls — the widest waterfall on Earth, where the mile-wide Zambezi River runs into the canyon at the country's border with Zimbabwe — we walked through the markets where local crafters sold wooden sculptures of animals and other knick-knacks. Dad told me not to look at the large wooden tribal masks. Some were taller than me. He explained: "They symbolize evil spirits."

The few United States dollars my parents gave me went a long way at the market, and one day I bought a necklace with a white pendant on it carved from cow bone. The pendant was a coiled snake-like creature. I showed it to Dad. He grabbed it and threw it away.

"Alex," he said through gritted teeth, "Never buy that again."

He said the pendant was an idol, a false god. He said the people in the area believed that a snake god lived in the Zambezi River. "You know what that means, snake god?"

I understood. The Devil.

Years later, I would learn that Dad was conflating, intentionally or otherwise, two wildly different myths. The snake god of the Zambezi was Nyami Nyami, not Satan. Nyami Nyami has a fish head and snake body with large fangs. As symbols of the Zambezi river, the pendants were often purchased by thrill-seekers from rich countries looking to canoe the deadly rapids at the base of the Falls.

But when I was a child, Nyami Nyami was nameless, and the pendants in the market were terrifying. More importantly, they were my first evidence of a challenge to god's authority. My god, an all-powerful force, was threatened, or at least angered, by something I could fit in my hand.

Real questions came later — Zambia was simply where they started simmering in my mind. Why didn't god just destroy the pendants? If Africa was in need of god's message — if we had to go into the villages to spread his word — why did god need some people from rural Georgia to do this? If so, what were the limits of his power? Why did he have such a foothold at home but not in Africa?

I learned what *gay* meant in a Baptist church back in America. I had heard the word before. It was a playground word, something like *cooties*, a word my classmates — mostly the guys — called each other when one of them dropped a ball or did something annoying. I thought it meant *stupid*.

Stupid gay cooties. That's what I now have.

One day, a boy my age raised his hand in Sunday school and asked the teacher, Miss Terry — matronly, sweetly Southern — if gay people go to hell. Miss Terry was visibly discomforted by the question and her face darkened. She asked if anyone knew what gay meant. Some kids raised their hands. Miss Terry then explained: gay is what happens when two men are together the way boys and girls are supposed to be.

I am how I am supposed to be.

The innocence of her explanation, the gentleness of it, was followed by her brutal confirmation: being gay is a sin, and gay people must ask god for forgiveness. She didn't go so far as to say we go to hell, but she didn't have to — her kind face, transformed by the sickness of belief, said what she couldn't: that some among us were meant to burn.

Even after my family permanently moved back to the United States, we continued visiting Zambia every few years. Throughout middle school and high school, I went on mission trips to Zambia, doing pretty much what my parents did while we lived there — spreading the word — and sometimes we built storage buildings or painted the walls of orphanages. But for one night on every trip, the team went to a village in the bush, taking along a white bedsheet and a projector, and played a film about the life of Christ. After the film, a local pastor from the area shouted to the hundreds of people gathered in their native tongues — Tonga, Bemba, Lozi — calling them to come forward and be saved.

I still speak in tongues, with tongues.

I was always one to offer up prayers, or I watched as others tried to. In the dead of night, the African stars above us, I put my hands on them and they on me, and though we did not speak the same language, we knew what prayer looked and felt like, and these nights were among the most beautiful experiences of my life. That was what faith once felt like.

But in high school, I was increasingly aware that I was carrying around a lie — that I did not believe, and worse, I was not what others thought I was. I was camouflaged, a snake in the tree.

I am deadly.

When I learned that god was threatened by *gay* even more violently than a tiny African god, he withered in size — fell down into my pocket, rattled about with a bit of cow bone. The Zambian people's cosmology of protective or malevolent spirits, their rites to the dead, seemed more sensible and truer while the sermons and megachurches I attended became increasingly cruel and embarrassing.

Gay, a word evenly matched in sound and syllable, felt more dangerous than god. I wanted knowledge and sought it. What I found was a new religion, one in which I was worshiped instead.

I am cow bone. I am a false god.

I felt free, finally, powerful, dangerous. Gay was forbidden fruit on my tongue.

Xmas

My first Christmas as an HIV-positive man was rough. I was suicidal, and to make things worse, I worked at a restaurant. I attended the host desk; I was a host in so many ways. Whenever an unhappy guest complained about their table or the atmosphere, I was tempted to say, "You're the reason I won't be alive tomorrow, and I want you to live with that." Dramatic, but that's just how heavy my world felt and how close I was to collapse. I was an angry host.

I am an angry host.

I'm not sure when dying started to look less like a concept and more like something to do on an idle afternoon, but I knew when it was time to call someone. I started calling suicide hotlines. I did this four or five times. Each person talked to me for about an hour, and the calls always made me feel better. Theirs was a thankless job.

The talks helped me survive the few days that followed, but I couldn't see anything long-term for me. The calls did not help me answer real questions, ones most people have. *Why undertake this business, life?* The people on the phone said I was brave and made sure I wasn't about to harm myself — or at least they reached a point where they felt comfortable not calling 911 — but I was still empty, no real reason for living.

I wanted life to justify itself. Life provides no built-in purpose, no implicit value — if anything, it fails, unsustainable until it reaches ruin. I would die someday. Why not then?

How about now?

I don't know how close I was to the edge, but the hardest point came one day after work when it was raining. I parked in the driveway and sat in my car, thinking and feeling nothing, watching the silvery rain slide down my windshield.

Mercury.

I was crashing over winter break from college in a friend's apartment while she was visiting her family, and a primary reason I didn't do it then was because she was a kind person. I didn't want to traumatize her by hanging myself in her bathroom. Even at the end, I wanted to be considerate. But it would be easy, and in a few moments, her trauma would no longer be my concern. Someone else's problem: *that's me, finally*.

I could take a fistful of pills with the stinging taste of bourbon or attach my gorgeous brown leather belt to the sturdy pipe over her clawfoot tub. It was a logical decision, really.

Soon, my manager at the restaurant gathered everyone together and said that, based on our reservation schedule, the holidays would be busy, and we had to be prepared for several large parties. At that moment, I truly doubted my ability to make it to January. With my holiday work schedule, I could only go to my parents' farm on Christmas morning, and I would have to drive back to town the next day. I was relieved, as I was certain my parents would notice something different about me the moment I walked in the door. Strangers may not be able to see HIV floating through a body, but I was certain that parents had something instinctual that would signal them when their children were sick — like dogs smelling cancer.

I got off early on Christmas Eve and went to the town's only gay club. My friend, a drag queen named Parfait, joined me. I wore a naughty reindeer costume — underwear and felt antlers — while Parfait wore a latex catsuit with devil horns *for the baby Jesus*.

We drank all night. I wailed *Runaround Sue* and *Hallelujah* into the karaoke mic at the back of the bar. Everyone clapped. I don't really recall these people. They were the other local men who had no one to go home to, whose parents were dead or might as well be. And, for that moment, we were gathered together on a Christmas island of misfit toys, attempting to lick each other's wounds. The white-haired, foul-mouthed bartender slung drinks strong and let us be merry. No one wanted to fuck. We hugged and laughed like brothers, sang carols and held hands. All the local drag queens served terrifying holiday realness. It was campy and warm, and everything was perfect because we had each found an us for one night. The next morning, in the sharp light of dawn, still coming out from my drunken fog, I drove north to my family's 500-acre farm.

+ + +

Somehow, Dad had become a hugger. He started doing this in my second year of college. I hugged him delicately, like I was hugging a bull who could hurt me. When I was little, everyone said I looked like him, but I never saw it. I am adopted, and these comments often made me wonder if my adoptive Dad was actually my biological father.

I wonder, still.

Our characters have always been similar. We're brutish, bull-headed, convinced of our own moral correctness. But our ideologies took opposite trajectories long ago. More than politics, our orientations to the world just never aligned. I pointed to dim or shooting stars when navigating life. Dad was locked on to one with singular focus. The light of our love did not always connect across our great divide, but it was always there, a quiet signal in the night. Our love intersected when and where it mattered most.

When I have thought about our deaths, I've imagined them being profoundly different. I see him dying in a field at dusk after a day's hard work with little purple field flowers blooming at his feet. I wish I could die like that. I suspect his death will simply happen with dignity, while I will live through each moment of mine.

That's what happens to people like me, right?

He hugged me when I arrived home, and in that hug, I was certain I would die first, and however I did it, it would not be as grand as his passage from the world. An angel would swoop down and carry him away in a chariot of fire. I would simply fade.

My father's strength was cultivated by mid-Georgia farmers, men who worked at the quarry and the sock mill. My strength — like most of my features — was hollow and superficial. I took supplements and counted protein grams, and even with hours in the gym, I couldn't do anything very practical with my body except fuck for money. On other, more traditional work fronts, I had the muscle but lacked his finesse, his understanding of textures and tools, how things cut and screw and break. Dad was a surgeon, and he operated with the same cocksure precision he brought to every farm task, from fixing a tractor to building an irrigation system. In his mind, the world was something to be taken apart and understood according to fixed laws and clear lines. That's where I did not belong. I was fluid, in flux; I was blurred, just passing through before passing on.

On these trips home, he always told me to come home more, because he missed me. But I wasn't sure which version of me he missed, which memory played in his mind. Somehow, I inherited his rage and intelligence and stubbornness, and as adults, that has left little space for building forts or playing in the water hose or whatever else we used to do. He was a Southern Baptist and I believed in nothing, mostly. He was Republican, I was Democrat. He was country, I was city. He was mechanical, I was *the schizophrenic artist in the family*, which was actually how he sometimes introduced me to people when I was younger. And like true believers both, we each were unrelenting and locked to what we knew was sacred truth. He made me this way and I was proud of the ways I did not compromise, and proud of the ways he did not, either. I never wanted him to relent for a moment. Who would I be without him? *Surely, not me.*

Maybe, in the end, that's what a father must be: a standard to beat against. A marker to measure difference. A rock upon which either to build or crash.

+ + +

We did Christmas. It was just my parents and my sister Jo, no cousins or aunts present. I never remember Christmas beyond its generic rituals — not the minutia, just the feeling — but I remember that year was tense. Dad began his interrogation as soon as I walked in the door: "How is school?" "Tell me about your classes." "What are your plans for after college?"

Classes were hard because writing was hard. I didn't have a plan for after school, but I couldn't say that. My life plan did not extend beyond December, because I was ready to die. I could not say anything about drag queens or glow-in-the-dark paint parties or the men I was fucking or HIV. And with those details — my life — untouchable, what else was there to say during Christmas with straight people?

We fell, as we always did, to a neutral topic — the projects around the farm that needed working on. My parents don't know how to sit still and will never retire. They build things, re-do things. A barn, a treehouse. They are intelligent, and they believe *idle hands are the devil's workshop.*

Dad tried sports. "Alex, you need to know about this game on right now," he said. "All your friends at school will be talking about it and you really need to know about it."

All my friends would not be talking about it. The last talk I had with my friends was about hot topics like *colonialists* and *the patriarchy*, which we somehow decided had been diluted by white elitist liberalism and no longer had any real meaning. The word patriarchy, in particular, ruffled my friend Aster. "I think we need to find a new word," she said, setting down her glass of wine. Everyone at the table was white and privileged. "Of course, patriarchy is a problem and must be talked about, but I think it's also oversimplified and when anyone says it — especially when I say it as a woman — people just stop listening." I suppose this was my sort of sport, along with constant training for the butthole Olympics.

Win the goddamn gold, Alex. Go big or go home.

I offered Dad this: "I learned my school has a mascot. For the soccer team."

"What's the mascot?"

"The bees! I just found out."

"Alex, you've been there *four years*."

I thought bees were great. They die by massive trauma after stinging, leaving their guts behind in honor of their last stand.

+ + +

After dinner, I carried my suitcase upstairs to my old bedroom. The room was unchanged, untouched, but I was different. It seemed tiny, and I was a ghost walking through my past life. When I've told people I grew up on a farm, raised by two wealthy doctors, they say it sounds idyllic. It was not when I was growing up, though it became so. I liked going home. But it only became bearable after I learned more about the world beyond the farm, after I had the orgies and the sin and pop culture and other Queer people and all the stuff I didn't believe could possibly exist when I lived there.

The most controversial books on my shelf had been put in the closet, which I thought funny because they missed a few. *Naked Lunch* and *Lolita*

... light of my life, fire of my loins. My sin, my soul.

I stepped into my old bathroom. This was where I first studied my body and knew I wanted to touch other bodies like mine. In the mirror, I still felt like a child, but I was becoming a man, a full-grown faggot, a slut with HIV. I wished my younger self could see me like this, naked with a few tattoos appearing across my skin. That little boy would not believe his eyes. He would giggle and be shy and try so hard to impress me. But I did not feel proud or handsome. I still felt like I was a performance, and as an infected person, I still felt that no one would want to touch me.

This is really what I believed — and I was wrong, of course. I know that now. But it's strange to return from isolation back to isolation, untouchable to untouchable, in the same little bathroom and the same house, to believe, thanks to different sins — the sin of being gay and the sin of sex — that I was cut off from the world. I had a stab of beauty — I knew that — and I was learning how to use it. But I understood that I would always be chasing that enviable gay commodity, and HIV was so new to me then that I believed my looks were the only thing that could save me.

I started the shower. The piping in the house was loud and my parents in their bedroom below could hear the exact moment I started the water and the moment I stopped it, which always felt like they were listening in. I was never fucked at the farm, so I never douched out my hole in the shower.

When I arrived at college, I didn't know how to douche. I thought gay men just fucked shit. But after four years, douching had become a tired ritual, like brushing my teeth, just something one does. I wondered if my parents knew I did this.

What would they think? Did they know words like *top* and *bottom*? Perhaps they imagined gay men as hive-minded worker ants, maniacally versatile, fucking and getting fucked equally in large, underground burrows and hallways. That image wasn't completely off, but Mom, Dad: some guys are stallions, and some are mares. You know which one I am now.

The last time my father talked to me about gay sex — the night I was confronted about my sexuality, the worst night of my life — he said, "It's *poop*, Alex. That's all it is. *Poop.*"

He was furious. He took a breath and said, "You'll grow up and live in some apartment that smells like stool, and you won't even notice it, because you'll live in it."

I have never felt so ashamed in my life. At that moment, I didn't know anything about gay sex and believed he was telling me the truth. He was my parent, so I trusted his word. Poop was waiting for me. My life would be poop. In some ways, he would end up being right, as he has been about so much.

My fights with him were my core ingredient — the thing most responsible for who and what I became. His face, which by that Christmas was aged and gray and gentle, could just as easily transform in my memory, revert course. I could close my eyes and watch his skin redden and his eyes become glassy. He could clench his jaw and stand over me — impossibly strong.

When I was little and misbehaved, he would hold me down on the floor and grip my face in his hands, hold his face inches from mine, his hand squeezing my cheeks and jaw. He held my head in place so I had to look up at him, and in a moment I could be there again, my full field of vision in his face, and feel his spit splash on my cheek as he said, "Apologize to your mother!" or something like that. I must have just sassed her or kicked something or did something bad, whatever kids do. I have never been so terrified of someone as I was of him.

Now, I love men who hold me down, choke me, spit in my face. I crave their brutality, their discipline. I like being told what to do. I am my father's faggot. I chase daddies, doms, angry fuckers. I am a masochist. The hurt is male power impacting my body.

This is my body, broken for you.

His fury was right. His fury was love. And his love was a beast. Here I was, home for the holidays, with HIV.

Dad never hit me or kicked me out of the house. His love was violent and filled with moral fury, but it was still love. A child can't see that, and as an adult, I have remained confused by that simple truth. More than a father, he was a man. Age had softened him, made him kinder, perhaps even a little defeated. I was not an easy son to have.

I am an easy son to have. Spit. Shove.

Dad found religion the way many people do — through suffering and abandonment. His father left his mother, my grandmother, when he was just a boy. There were other losses, too, but nobody spoke of them. I didn't know my father's full life, like he knew mine. Without knowing who he was and who he is, it was harder to understand him as a full and flawed man.

My cousins remembered Dad as the joking, irreligious prankster, the fun uncle. When I started asking questions, I was told that my sister and I were one or two years old when he changed. He started talking about the Bible and the Book of Revelation and attending religious conferences, all of which made my cousins uncomfortable. And that was the birth of the man I've known all my life. And now that I'm an adult — and a fighter — I find myself wanting to protect my dad the way he wanted to protect me. He had years of rage. I had years of resentment. We had years of conflict. And we always had years of love.

He always joked at family gatherings about Mom leaving him. "I'll give her everything," he says, grinning as if this was funny. "I'll just drive away with the Jeep and the dog."

Mom always waved the joke away, but I knew — and she knew — that it was not a joke. He always expected her to walk out as others have walked out on him. As I did. I was the difficult son of a difficult man.

I think that Christmas was the first time I tried to understand my father, and it didn't happen because of anything he said or did. It happened because I was questioning my own life, weighing its options, and deciding if I wanted to die before ever coming to a kind of resolution with him. So much needed to be said between us, and if I ended things, I would never be able to say them.

+ + +

In a way, he was right. My sex life was poop. I cleaned it out of me and pushed it down the drain and prevented it from appearing when I got fucked. I don't live in that shit-smelling apartment, but some gay households have showers that smell faintly of shit from all the frequent douching. And even with this truth, I had and still have no kind of apology to offer, because I am beyond shame. We play with our bodies. We fuck buttholes. Sometimes there is poop. But we are free and just exactly as we are made to be.

In the shower that Christmas night, I got on my hands and knees and put my ear to the floor. I did the same throughout high school, and this would be the last time I did it. Directly below me was the hallway between my parents' bedroom and bathroom and I could hear their footsteps; they were talking, as married people do at the end of a day. I could never hear them clearly but every now and then a word, or something that sounded like a word, came through.

Sins or since. Offenses or fences.

My mother was probably in her white bathrobe, seated and beautiful without makeup, like an orchid. When my sister and I went to college, she started scrapbooking our lives, collecting report cards, drawings, and photographs in large binders. I don't think she ever made it past the high school years for me, and I didn't know how she could go much further. She didn't know much of the rest.

At that moment, two words came through the floor of the shower: *tomorrow, engine.* Maybe Dad had to check the tractor engine tomorrow. And I considered those two words, their simple clarity, the gifts of that year. I was shocked at how clearly I heard them through the floor. They meant nothing to me, they were just words, but by hearing them, I felt like I was above my parents, watching over them.

And that made me incredibly sad. Without me, who would watch over them, listen in on their conversations, cause a stir to force discussion? Would this shower go empty? Would they never again hear the pipes rumble in their ceiling? I was sad with the thing that still breaks my heart, even now, years after I decided to keep living: the fact that I have never been able to love or understand my parents enough.

They provided me with a life, though I don't know who exactly gave me life. I've benefited from thousands of meals, incalculable amounts of money, unending patience, ceaseless love. And, somehow, I demanded they be better, that they be people other than who they are. As straight, Christian people, they could not help most of what comes with that lifestyle choice. I've wondered how they can live in that box and the constraints of it. They've wondered how I will survive outside of it.

At that moment in the shower, I was filled with something like sympathy. They were given a child they did not understand. I lied and lashed out. And even in their confusion and conviction, they loved me because they did not know how to do anything else. During that brief Christmas visit, they asked me to come home more. It was love and only love that made them try to hold on to me.

I whispered down a confession through the drainpipe that they were doing a good job, and that I was holding out on them. It was a sort of prayer, I guess, or maybe an apology padded in hope. Maybe it reached them through the floor, but I doubt it.

Airport

I met Miguel a year after I tested positive. He transferred to my college from a school in Caracas. I was a senior and he was a sophomore, and I was graduating in a few months, so we knew our relationship was over before it started. We had no money, so dates meant going to the dining hall and pretending to buy each other dinner. But one night he made me cornflower arepas, his favorite dish from home, and they were the most delicious thing I'd eaten.

By that point, I had healed a bit from my HIV diagnosis and started learning my history. I discovered the story of AIDS in America after I realized I would not die from it. After some research, I learned that AIDS killed some incredibly cool people. I was part of a club of great artists and activists. I was already framing my diagnosis as a bisector, a line cutting my life in two. Everything before it was preamble. My past life no longer mattered. I was a new thing, living on borrowed time, my life won by faggots who lived before me.

Miguel was not afraid of HIV. He had a thing for daddies and had fucked older guys who were positive. When he fucked me, he insisted on using condoms, and I said okay. He was a dominant top, and he was the first man I met who truly went ravenous over ass.

His brown eyes were dog-like when he fucked, dazed and hungry. He looked down at me, lifting his chin, and I remember his sweat beading along his long, dark eyebrows. He often snorted and growled when he came.

Our playful courtship was enhanced by the understanding that this would be brief. Every day together was our last.

One day I brought him to the farm to meet my parents. The trip was a last-minute event — flights were timed inconveniently, and he needed a place to crash for two days. I was planning a visit to the farm for a family gathering and told him to tag along. Suggesting this, I knew I was playing with fire. He knew about my Dad and our fights, but he was fearless and said *okay*.

I called Dad to ask if this was acceptable. He said, "Of course," which really bothered me. Where was his fury?

Months prior, on another visit to the farm, Dad repeated his belief that my sexuality was the work of evil spirits. Even though I half-suspected this was true, and the Devil was loads of fun, I hated his view that the most beautiful part of my life was not even mine — that it could be stripped from me with just a little drop of Christ's blood.

During that fight, I threw a suitcase at him from the second-floor balcony, followed by a can of bug spray. In my defense, the suitcase was empty, and my aim was terrible, so the bug spray exploded upon impact somewhere behind him in the kitchen.

Miguel thought this story was funny. He didn't realize that I really wanted to hurt Dad at that moment. I don't recall ever hating Dad so much as I did then. That fight was the first and last time I dragged from memory the things he had said previously.

"I never said that." And, so, I started throwing things.

You'll die of AIDS before you're thirty.

It's poop, Alex.

Dad knew nothing of my HIV. No one in my family did. This secret would go to my grave.

Miguel's presence would keep us from fighting like that again. Southern people can be counted upon to deliver the veneer of hospitality even when they hate you.

"They'll make you sleep in the guest bedroom," I told him.

"That's fine."

"Is it? We sleep together all the time. We're adults."

"Alex, please don't make it a fight."

Miguel was gentler than I was. I held him every night, kissing his neck, his hair. We both knew this thing between us was doomed, but we kept up hope. Maybe it would last. I needed it to last.

I wanted him to see the house in the woods where I used to live. I was proud of the land. Turning off the road into a dense pine forest gave me the feeling of having retreated, returned to my origins, and to Miguel, this was my home — the place I was from. I didn't have the words to tell him it wasn't. My real home was the warm space beside him on the bed, and I wondered what would happen to me when it was gone.

I parked the car in my parents' driveway. Miguel rubbed my shoulder. "Alex, I love you, but I need you to relax. You are now making *me* nervous."

Dad walked out of the house to greet us. I introduced Miguel and watched the men shake hands. Miguel had a silver eyebrow piercing and nose ring, and I saw these for the first time as insurrections.

Dad asked, "How was the drive?"

Miguel ignored his question. "This place is beautiful! The trees are beautiful! Oh my god! What kind of trees are these? Look at the dog! Hello dog!" and on and on. When Miguel became excited, his words tumbled over each other, occasionally dipping into Spanish. He often lost his place in sentences and had to start again, and it was wondrous to behold.

He was not afraid of Dad, and I wished I could be like him. But I wasn't. I walked in front of Miguel, wary, ready to bite. As my father gave a tour of the house and grounds, I tried signaling to Miguel for him to be careful. He didn't know who this man could be.

In the house, Mom swept the floor and talked in her loud *everything is okay!* voice. My sister Jo moved through the kitchen angrily preparing casseroles. Mom shouted, "I hope you're hungry!" and this was the moment when it became a TV sitcom. Everything was ready, a full presentation. My sister stood in the middle of the room and said, "Hey brother!" as she does. Other family members arrived, my aunt and cousins. It was a big meal, a big gathering, and it happened perfectly in every way. I could not have asked for a better visit. I felt it would close with smooth jazz playing and everyone laughing around the table.

I pulled Miguel to the porch and asked, "Are you okay? Has anyone said anything to you?"

"Alex, everyone is so nice. The only one here with an issue is you."

"I'm the one with an issue? These people are cruel."

We looked through the window into the kitchen. Dad was gently handing out slices of pecan pie to everyone.

I took Miguel for an ATV ride through the woods. Far from the house, we kissed against a tree. I unbuckled his pants and knelt in the dirt. His caramel-colored dick had the flavor of a long day on it. It tasted good, better than most I've sucked. His foreskin and tip had a distinct, sweet flavor in them. The shaft curved strongly to the right, so if I wanted to deep-throat, I had to tilt my head and take it sideways.

"This feels like a porno," he said.

I tried to say *yeah* but just choked.

Back at the house, my sister asked Miguel about his tattoos. He was an illustration major, so he drew most of them. Jo asked to see more of his work, and he pulled up his portfolio on his phone. Miguel created bright, pastel, slightly cartoonish pictures of Nordic gods and astronauts and chubby men in underwear. His colorful style was great for a magazine cover, and years later, he landed an excellent job with a big company in San Francisco.

I could not tell if my family cared. He drew the tattoo on his forearm — a Mason jar filled with flowers — and explained that his sister and mother had the same one. They all got it together, their mark of kinship.

My sister laughed. "Can you imagine *us* doing that!" But it wasn't a joke, not really. We just weren't that kind of family.

The next morning, I drove Miguel to the airport so he could fly back to Venezuela and be with his family. "I think you are being unfair, Alex," he said.

"Okay."

"When we were driving down, I wasn't sure I could like your dad because of the things he said to you. But Alex, I liked your dad."

"I want us to talk about something else."

Not everyone gets the chance to be with someone better than themselves, but I was given that with Miguel, and I dreamed that, if he stayed with me, we would figure all this out, this mystery between me and my parents. He would give me the right words to say to them.

I dropped him off at the airport and he was gone. His absence echoed. The temperature dropped. This man — someone who bent for others, accepted slights and injuries — was gone and I was left in my world. I was the source of slights and injuries, and he endured them. I had already cheated on him once and he had stupidly, foolishly forgiven me.

Driving back to my college dorm in Savannah, I knew something significant had happened in my life, but I didn't want to quantify it. I didn't dare see the visit as the end of a battle. I was still angry. By bringing him to the farm, he became evidence to my parents — to Dad — that I was fucking a man. I wished privately that Dad could see what Miguel did to me, see my hands tied with neckties to the bedframe. I felt Miguel's thick curve in my butthole, and when he roared, I roared. Together, our sex was exploratory and mighty. If nothing else, I hoped Dad would see the athleticism in what we did and know that I was, if nothing else, not a weakling.

The visit was over, with no problems. It went as well as any taking-home-the-boyfriend story could have gone. The only tense moment came when Miguel was sitting with Dad at the dining room table and my father asked, "Do you ever get stopped at the airport because of how you look?"

"Like, how do you mean?"

"You don't look strictly American."

I was standing in the pantry, out of sight, holding my breath.

"Yes, but I'm from South America, not the Middle East. I don't understand." Miguel did not sound angry, just genuinely confused.

"I know, I know," Dad said, a hint of exasperation in his voice. He was a surgeon, so I presumed he knew the difference between Venezuela and Iran. "I just meant with the beard and the piercings."

Miguel actually laughed. "No, I never get stopped in the airport." He didn't say that he had to live in fear of racial profiling and getting harassed by American cops.

The conversation drifted to Venezuela. Miguel told everyone about the violence there, how some of his friends got kidnapped and held for ransom, how he never stopped at stop signs because thieves might run out, shoot him, and steal the car.

"Say what you want about America," Mom said. "At least you can stop at a stop sign here!"

Miguel realized the conversation had backfired. "Yeah, but Venezuela is so beautiful. I think it's more beautiful than America." He showed my parents pictures of the view from the porch of his family home, which appeared to be built on the side of a mountain, overlooking a lush green valley.

Dad scratched his head, his telltale sign of frustration. I watched him. But he said nothing, and I said nothing. He and Miguel talked, asked questions of each other. I realized Miguel was better at this. He was being a better son than I could be.

I liked the tales of Miguel's country and his life before coming to the United States, but I did not contextualize them or understand the politics — of his country or mine — as I had not fully placed myself or my parents into the American political ethos. My identity as a faggot was not politicized yet. It would be soon.

As I drove through the Georgia countryside, I thought about my parents and their lives between these visits, how empty the house must feel without my sister and me in it. We were both in college and finishing our degrees. They feared, perhaps, what I would become — silence, an unanswered phone call. I imagined them years in the future, their hair white, sadly setting down the phone, having missed me again. They did not deserve that, but I knew my nature. They raised a man unable to stay.

Somewhere overhead, Miguel was barreling through the air on his way to a country I've never seen. His parents told him this visit would likely be his last. Venezuela was becoming too dangerous. His sister had moved to Panama and his parents were following her soon.

What is it like to go home for the last time?

At that moment, I would have given anything to fly south. I would alight down to his house on the mountain and sit down with his family to a big meal, arepas and pastelitos, and we would laugh around the table. Music would play. I would talk to his parents, get to know them, and be absolved of any need to actually know mine.

Faithless

I was in the student computer lab at college reading about female infanticide in China. I don't remember the full article, just one story included in it: a taxi driver in Shanghai accidentally backed over a five-year-old girl and heard her crying. He chose to back over her again and kill her because he knew this would be cheaper than paying for her medical bills.

The author of the article cited this story as one example of the harmful effects of one-child and two-child policies, which had reportedly created a culture in which female infants were, to some extent, expendable. But I had stopped reading by then, because I could hear her, the girl, her sobs. The sound of her crying under a tire haunted me all day.

Did her bones pop when crushed?

I've always been a philosophy nerd and interested in religion, and at the time, I believed in god, or at least my version of him. What was he telling me? I thought about the girl, the dull thud of her being hit and crunched, her last moments of pain.

I was a deist, and a deist would say her life was ferried into existence by an omniscient being who, at the moment of her birth, knew a brutal death was coming five years later. And she was just one person to die, one of so many. Why did her death — her life — matter?

+ + +

Is God willing to prevent evil, but not able? Then he is not omnipotent.

When I was about ten, I asked Dad for information about angels and demons. We were riding in his Jeep, running an errand, and I wanted to know if angels and demons could be seen, observed.

"Of *course*," he said in his preaching voice, irritation mixed with excitement, the same voice I use now when I show off what I know. "Remember those witch doctors in Africa? They were possessed by demons."

"But how will I be able to tell when someone's a demon?"

I wanted to know the signs. How could I discern between demoniacs and people who were just mean? Some of my classmates were up for consideration.

I never got these details, and years later, after the bent little prissy in me was revealed for what it was, he explained that demons and evil forces were at least partially responsible for homosexuality. He conceded, in the middle of our fight, that the impulse for faggotry probably sits latent, dormant, inside many men, like cancers in remission, and that these sicknesses only become symptomatic when we turn away from god and are *given to the sinful desires of our hearts*. He was quoting a passage from the Book of Romans. He added that demons and evil spirits encourage this slippage, pushing curious boys like me into the dark — into something that is, by his own admission, part of the natural self.

When he told me that, I remembered our unfinished talk in the Jeep so many years ago and wondered if he avoided answering the question because he suspected even then what I was, what I would become. He couldn't or wouldn't say what he knew.

Just look in the mirror.

When I started to understand what I was, I knew that my faith clashed with my dreams in the shower about guys on my football team. James, a tall, blonde left tackle, was a prankster and liked getting naked and pulling out his junk. He had big, floppy blonde balls and a big dick and talked about it often. During trips to away football games, he pulled out his beautiful balls and rested them gently on teammates' faces when they fell asleep on the bus. All I wanted was to be his victim.

I knew that the god of my Baptist church did not like these thoughts about James' balls, despite being the alleged designer of them. But I had a way out of this predicament. I could turn away from my thoughts, ask god for help, and one day they would just vanish. Because god could do anything.

+ + +

Is he able, but not willing? Then he is malevolent.

Some religious Queers like to contest the claim that our lifestyles clash with Christianity. They say the historic abuses of homos by Christians are the result of misguided church policy or social prejudice, not divine mandate. This is little more than a semantic argument. On a practical level, I am being asked to distinguish between cruelty enacted by people and cruelty enacted by people on god's orders. Either way, it's still cruelty.

From a young age, I wanted to be a pastor. I liked reading the Bible and learning its applications, and history. I couldn't do math or catch a football, but I could work my mind around the minutia of doctrine. That conversation with Dad in his Jeep was one of many talks we had like that, and most of the time, he patiently answered my questions, opening his leather Bible and guiding me to answers in the text. His Bible was worn and beautiful, filled with loose pages, notes, and scribbles. It was permanently bent from being stuffed in his back pocket for days on end.

My father is an objectively brilliant man, and he encouraged me to think deeply, recognize problems in the world, and think about things that others likely didn't. We shared a seriousness about religion that my mother and sister did not, which felt like he and I were on a holy mission, united against the forces of evil in the heavenly realms.

But in middle school, I made the mistake of asking questions about Catholics, and for the first time, my questions were discouraged. I thought Catholics were mysterious and cool. I didn't want to be Catholic, just to know more about them. One day, when I was about fourteen, I asked my parents to buy me some Catholic books at a Christian bookstore we liked to visit. They told me to put them back.

Their efforts backfired. I was a curious teenager. After that, every religious concept except Southern Baptist Christianity was fascinating. In bookstores, I pored through books on Greek mythology and art, mostly for the nude sculptures and penises, but they led me to a new world of wondrous fable, too.

One day my parents reluctantly bought me a book of illustrated world myths. The front cover featured an illustration of the Greek myth of Prometheus, the fire thief, so they must have assumed the book was filled with old Greek mythology — obvious fairy tales. But when I got home, I found the book also contained Christian stories like "Noah and the Ark," "Jonah and the Whale," and so on. That book was one of the most powerful things to drop into my life. Its illustrations were clearly made to entertain kids, but its implications were profound. By presenting Bible stories alongside "Theseus and the Minotaur," it did one of two things: it either made stories I was supposed to believe in look flimsier, or it made the story of Odin carving the first humans out of driftwood more plausible.

For me, it did both.

There were similarities between stories, even ones from wildly different cultures, and I came to a logical crossroads: if various cultures had common myths, then was Christianity just one interpretation of a more universal truth? And what if there was a better interpretation?

This wicked little idea was working through my head when my family returned to Zambia during the summer before my junior year of high school. It was just a two-week trip to visit a Christian orphanage, but I was told we'd be sharing the guest house with another visiting group — an aggregate of local churchgoers from across the Deep South. And one of them was a guy on my varsity football team.

At first, I didn't believe it. He was a troublemaker. He was bad. I now think he just wanted an adventure, and his parents thought he couldn't get in much trouble on a mission trip. *It might even be good for him.*

It was good for me.

I fell hard. We stayed up late talking in the common room of the guesthouse after everyone was asleep. Once, he asked me to hand him his towel through the curtain after he showered, feeding me glimpses of his body. He liked the attention. We often disappeared from the group, ran up the hill at the front of the compound, and sat on the rocks, looking out at the valley below us. In the distance, we could see smoke from village fires and, even further, the steam rising from Victoria Falls over miles of elephant grass.

One day, while we were up there, he told me to stand on his shoes. I obeyed. He put his arms around me, and I put mine around him. We danced, stiff-legged, silly, smelling each other, permitted only to be this close because it was a joke, a challenge: how long could we keep balance, hopping around on shared feet? It only lasted a few seconds, but in those seconds, his body won my struggle. My god became gay with one dance.

Over the next few days, I was too obvious with my affections for him, and when my teammate left, I started crying in front of all the adults like a schoolgirl dumped on prom night. They were watching and I didn't care. They hung their heads, saying nothing.

The night we arrived back in the United States, I was sitting in my bedroom, my bags still unpacked from the long journey returning me from Africa to the farm, when Dad walked in and said, "I think you're still dealing with this gay problem."

How did he not see god was the problem?

That's how the horrible night began.

+ + +

Is he both able and willing? Then whence cometh evil?

That night wasn't the end of my life as a believer, just as a closeted fag. Since the worst people to know my secret now knew it, to hell with my classmates: I told everybody.

The months that followed were probably the worst of my life, and I used my faith in god to get through them, praying as often as I could, even kneeling over a big family Bible. For privacy, I did this in my closet, unironically.

The time came for me to get a car and drive myself to school, but Dad said I could only do so once *the gay problem* was sorted out. So, he took me every week to speak with our pastor.

Bless the pastor's heart.

He wasn't a cruel one, not one of those fire-and-brimstone Baptist pastors people hear about. He was just inept. He was too meek, too Southern, tried too hard to be down-home and funny in his sermons, and never really got into the meat of the text. He quickly presented his arsenal — Bible verses allegedly condemning homosexuality — and I already knew all of them by heart. I actually didn't mind these talks, because they finally gave me a chance to talk to an adult about a subject I enjoyed. What really hurt was my parents' hope that these little chinwags would change me. I doubt they've ever grasped the irony that their efforts to get me back on track with god was the first irreparable crack in my ability to ever again be a Christian.

I started secretly reading (and, on more than one occasion, stealing) books about Buddhism. Then Islam, Judaism, shamanism, Wicca, mystery cults, and so on. I tried each religion on, tested ideas in my mind and mouth, happy to pray to this god or that. I even tried spellcasting with a rock and some dirt before giving up and feeling stupid. I discarded each approach, one after another, like boyfriends.

God needs to be as desirable as good dick.

I was floating in this murky, indecisive religious territory when I went to college. I occasionally told people I was pagan or called myself an "almost-Christian." But then I read about the five-year-old girl in China.

Years later, I would recall this story as the beginning of my atheism. But the truth is, atheism for me has always felt like a half-truth. At parties and in the beds of men I've fucked, it's been easier to call myself secular than say I'm simply a nemesis.

+ + +

Is he neither able nor willing? Then why call him God?

Some months after knowledge of the five-year-old girl came into my life, I tested positive, and the ugliness of a supreme being crystallized for me. In the bleakest days of AIDS, Christian pastors taught — and Christian adherents believed, and I suspect my parents believed — that the plague was judgment. Some HIV-positive people have told me god carried them through the dark years. God, who either through negligence or intention, slaughtered their friends and lovers.

No.

Atheism has served me better day-to-day because it's the kinder reality: animals dancing on a ball hurtling through space. Most days I believe in that world, but every now and then, I murmur an enraged prayer. They just slip out.

Where were you when I laid the foundations of the Earth?

Am I an atheist or just faithless? I've left most people who claimed ownership of me, so why not go bigger? In any case, I've always loved getting watched, and it would be a shame if my best nights were only witnessed by those who shared them with me — who slapped their balls across my face or stuffed them in my mouth. I've imagined the god of my parents watching me, too. With a body that can experience these things, I've even been tempted, when loads of semen are leaking from my destroyed butthole, to say thanks.

Oh god. Oh god. Yes!

S.F.

Sex was digitized by the time I met my Sir. In my freshman year of college, every gay man I knew had to contend with a brand-new technology: hookup apps. I went to college the year Grindr hit the Apple app store.

Four years later, the shorthand: I had to be *looking* or *DTF* (down to fuck). I had to present myself as something simple, a list of traits to be wanted or refused, and I learned to see other men this way, too.

'Sup? ParTy?

His name was Paul. His profile said he was into "kink, ink, and twink." We were both surprised by how close we lived to each other — I could walk to his house in under ten minutes — so we met at a Mexican restaurant around the corner. There I had my first discussion on fetishes and limits, things I would do and things I wouldn't. Mostly, I talked about things I wanted him to do to me.

He wanted a *submissive. A boy.*

It was me.

My general idea of BDSM — which stands for bondage, domination, sadism, and masochism, among other things — was something like the fuzzy pink handcuffs and ball gags I saw in the kitschy sex shop that the college kids snickered about. I knew I wanted to try that stuff — I had privately known for years — but Paul was a radicalizing force in my life by simply pulling it, and me, out of fantasy and into the heavy reality of his bedroom.

The first time we played, he tied my hands behind my back, then tied a thin rope around my testicles and started slapping them. Our first session grew into regular meetups, which led to a tender sexual relationship that lasted almost three years. When I tested positive for HIV, he held me like a lover, without any sexual expectation, only comfort. Savannah was my kink training ground.

Yes, Sir.
Please, Sir.
Thank you, Sir.

A Sir is the dominant playmate in kink and BDSM. I called Paul Sir, but others might have different names for their dominant playmates. For me at that time, Sir provided sex sessions and taught me how to play, slowly expanding my kink repertoire and my hole. The power dynamic we explored did not continue outside the bedroom. These titles and their expectations are all subjective, and others have Sirs who provide different experiences and do different things.

Sir took me out of my head and into my body. Getting used like a hole, a living sex toy, made me stop thinking. The result was like therapy. He tied me up, taped my mouth, hooded me, whipped me, spanked me, suspended me, cuffed me, and fucked me harder than I'd ever been fucked in my life, at least at that point. He fucked me so hard that I cried, and after I cried, I roared.

Hold me, Sir.

It was all consensual — in fact, he told me to ask for things and tell him what I wanted him to do. We were never dating, and outside our sessions, we had a warm and nurturing friendship. He took me to the gym, taught me how to exercise and lift weights, and ignited in me a passion for fitness that has never left. He cooked me dinner, gave me a place to sleep when I needed to get out of the dorms, and he encouraged my writing. I met his partner, walked his dog. We went out together, went to the bars, slept together, spooned. We talked about our pasts, and over time, my confessions leaked out — about my Dad, my fears — and his did too, but less generously. I understood there was trauma in him, and he understood there was some in me, and with this knowledge, he knew when to hit harder, and knew when to stop.

I needed him more than I could put into words. He took me to a place beyond — before? — language.

He was in his forties, hung, and very fit, and he told me immediately that he was a performer for a major fetish porn studio in San Francisco. He flew there often for shoots and considered the city his second home. For a college graduation present, he took me to my first Folsom Street Fair.

For the uninitiated, Folsom is billed as the world's largest leather and fetish event. For a weekend, several city blocks are crammed with people wearing leather, rubber, or nothing at all. Kink demonstrations — flogging, bondage — happened on little stages, or in the middle of the street. Onlookers crowded around a platform where a man had clothespins placed on every available inch of his body. Another man was tied to a pole and being brutally whipped by a woman in thigh-high latex heels. The red lashes crisscrossed down his back artfully, as if he had been branded by a chain-link fence.

Sir gave me my first leather harness, which is a construction of straps and buckles that leathermen usually wear over bare chests, transforming all adorned in them into some version of a restrained beast. He pulled me by the hand through porn sets and fetish parties where he had special access as a verified performer, a recognized face in the crowd. The day we left, I cried in the car.

"What was your favorite part?" he asked me.

"No one was afraid of my status."

It was true. Not one person turned me away because of my HIV.

That moment was when I chose to leave Miguel, my boyfriend in

Savannah, and move to this magical, strange, and dark city. The road to the airport dipped and climbed over San Francisco's hills in the deep dusk. It was hardly real, this city, and yet it was, and I wondered if this was the feeling gay men felt in decades past when they left their lives, ran away, settled here.

Shortly after we returned to Georgia, Sir lost his job — his employer in town found his porn — so we decided to move to San Francisco together.

Miguel thought this was a bad idea.

"I know you hate him," I said.

"I don't hate him. I just don't trust him."

Miguel only met my Sir a few times, and while he seemed understanding of what Sir did for me and how much I needed him, he was convinced there was something I should be wary of. But Miguel and I decided that if San Francisco didn't pull us apart, something else would. Our time had come to an end. We were students, and I was graduating. I was supposed to leave.

I kept saying this, *I'm supposed to leave,* and Miguel saw it, the unrooted thing in me, something he would never be able to contain, and one day he looked at me sadly in the shower, his brown eyes dipped into defeat, and I knew that was the moment he had let go.

We held each other on that last night, and in the morning, when Sir drove around the corner, I kissed Miguel, leaving him on the sidewalk, crying. I climbed in the car and was gone.

Ahead of us, the Wild West: the half of the country I knew nothing about except what I read in books and watched in movies. Kerouac made San Francisco feel dingy and brewing, dense and hard, all broken windows and lost people, but elsewhere — in what I knew from gay history — it seemed like a gay oasis of bellbottom pants and tight t-shirts, and I realized I was picturing the city in the seventies.

What was it now?

In Texas, the desert looked velvet, all burnt browns and soft pinks. Sir had some kind of living situation set up for us with a man who apparently operated his own private porn studio in his attic, and Sir hinted that this could be the beginning of my career as an adult film performer. The man who owned the house we'd be living in was named Michael.

"You're gonna love Michael! Michael is great. Although I have to warn you, Michael's a little odd." He was letting us live there rent-free. There was no risk, only reward.

I didn't care. I was gay, headed to San Francisco, and planned to never look back.

+ + +

Michael slept on a mattress in the living room because the rest of the house was bugged, or so he told us minutes after we walked in the door.

"Bugged by whom?"

"If you have to fuckin' ask, you're already fuckin' *screwed*."

Michael believed the United States was a puppet government controlled by the English Crown, that Hitler and the Holocaust were hoaxes, that all modern medicine caused cancer. Later, he would explain that vaccines contain microchips which turn people into government slaves, and that AIDS was fake — a Big Pharma conspiracy to sell pills, and worse, keep people sick. HIV, he explained, was a harmless passenger virus. "Everyone fuckin' has it," he said. "You don't see me taking any fuckin' pills."

Sir actually supported Michael's claims and, to my surprise, believed many of them. Both men encouraged me to go off my HIV meds.

"Alex, they're poison," Sir said one night, nearly in tears. "I'm scared for you."

They presented books and articles apparently confirming everything they told me, but that wasn't why I eventually believed them. I believed because I trusted Paul — Sir — and more than that, I loved him, and I knew he loved me. He was also an adult, and I was a 22-year-old kid.

His boy.

My break from HIV medication started in San Francisco and lasted more than a year.

Michael's fetish attic was a large, elaborate sex room — a dungeon, but on a third floor. Videos were once filmed there, but he never made the switch to digital content. Unsold VHS tapes filled every closet in the house. I suggested that he might want to convert his films to files that could be put on the Internet, where he could sell them. He told me the Internet is *made of gamma rays* that will *melt your fuckin' mind.*

Michael was in his fifties and had a hardcore kidnapping fetish. He regularly invited young men to the house, promising some bondage and isolation play, sessions that he assured would only last a few hours. Then he'd leave his victim locked in a dog cage for days. At any moment, I expected the police to knock on the door.

One day, I walked in the house talking on my phone. Michael screamed, "Put that goddamn thing away! I will never see it in this house again!"

I was confused until Sir said, "Alex, he means the phone."

Sir and I were instructed to limit our phone use to the guest bedroom, where we slept. "And you're killing your goddamn *brain* every time you use it."

It was quickly conveyed to me that the rent was not, in fact, free. Sexual favors were expected, but he said I had to lose some weight if I was going to be in his movies. When he learned I had some writing ability, he set me to editing stacks of stories he had written for what he described as an erotic website being developed. I knew it would never happen. The stories were entirely about rape, torture, kidnapping, even death.

I could go on about him, but he's neither that important nor complicated. He was just a bad person in San Francisco. There are bad people everywhere. I met other men there, men who gave me advice, gave me meals, took me to bed, showed me love, and gave me small glimpses of a wider gay world. Collectively the experience was, if nothing else, a dive into modern gay culture at the deep end of the pool. When I've told this story to gay men, they've said it's a very San Francisco story. I imagine most faggots have one like it: The city made me proud of who and what I was simply by not apologizing for anything. It let me fit in for the first time. And it refined my ability to detect bad situations. I've known others who didn't get out when they could.

+ + +

Sir laughed about Michael and called him a harmless eccentric.

"But he's not harmless," I said. "I don't feel safe."

"You don't feel safe? What do you mean, you don't feel safe? I'm here. You don't feel safe with me?"

And that was when I realized the truth.

No, I do not.

I was applying for jobs in the city, and one day Michael became violently angry that I wasn't moving fast enough through his hopelessly bad stories. I told him I had to apply for jobs in order to find work.

"But *this* is your goddamn job!" he said. "You work *here!*"

No, I do not.

"You fucking ungrateful son of a bitch! This is *my* house and I make the rules here!"

I nearly hit him. I don't know why I became so angry, so ready to topple a fifty-year-old man. I think it was simply the fear and the dark realization that I was financially and emotionally dependent on people I didn't trust. I screamed in his face. Michael looked at my Sir and said, "Get this fuckin' guy out of here."

I told Sir — I told Paul — *to buy me a plane ticket back to Savannah immediately.* It wasn't a request. He acted hurt, coquettish, petulant, and for the first time, I saw that he really had some serious problems. "Okay," he said. "Okay. Are you sure? Okay. Fine. Okay."

He bought me the ticket and drove me to the airport. In the security line, I looked back. He was still standing there, watching me, and he was crying, just as Miguel cried when I left, and I knew it was over between us. A jolt passed over me and I realized I would remember this moment. I was becoming good at leaving people behind.

+ + +

A year later, in another city, I got extremely sick and walked into a clinic where a gay man told me that everything I had been led to believe about my HIV — everything Sir believed — was wrong, and if I didn't start meds again, I would die. I restarted meds that day, and in the years since, I've almost never missed a daily dose. Of course, I did not know then how common and widespread some HIV conspiracy theories were, and my break from meds would become an illumination of how tenuous the understanding of perceived reality can be.

When that September came, I headed back to San Francisco and went to Folsom again. I set out when it was dark, and as the sun rose, the hills along my route looked blue. Beyond them was the stretch of open road through lemon groves. A few hours later, I rounded a corner and saw Castro Street sloping down the hill and felt a happy tug and wondered if this was what it felt like to come home.

Having done the bacchanal weekend once before, I had a better idea of how to do it on my own. Paul was there, but he was no longer Sir. We went to dinner and talked, but something in our eyes had changed. I was older and saw him for what he was — someone I had needed, then grown beyond. And I think he recognized the truth — I was kinkier than he was, wanted more than he signed up for. When I looked at him across the table, I saw a familiar, loving look, the eyes of a parent. He was afraid I would go too far.

I would. I will.

That night, I went to a party billed as "the best party of Folsom weekend," but when I got there, the place was empty. I walked from room to room wondering if I had made a mistake, shown up at the wrong venue. Some guys were making out on a deserted dance floor bathed in red light. No one else was there.

I turned to leave and must have looked confused because the doorman said, "Buddy, they're all in the back." He pointed me in the right direction. "Around the corner."

I hadn't noticed a black tarp hanging in a doorway. On the other side were hundreds of men walking through a dark sex maze. The music was not especially loud, which oddly added to the vibe of the space: all I could really hear were groans.

Oh, fuck.

The space was huge, and the play areas were sectioned off with tarps and metal fencing, and hidden in all the dark corners were slings and fuck tables and other sex furniture I had never seen before. I was over my head, not quite ready. It was, at first, too much. I walked through, watching, trying to convince myself that I belonged.

There was an open area of multitiered stages, arranged like terraces, where anyone could fuck for an audience. There I saw a lucky guy getting pounded on a leather bench. The top was magnificent. His body moved rhythmically, slowly, building up the hole's confidence before pulling out. Then, jackhammering: his hips slammed into the faceless hole, who, based on his sharp-pitched cries, was struggling to take it.

Amateur pig.

The bottom yelped, and there it was — the yelp, the holiest of sounds, the one I had made years earlier getting double fucked by my country buddies. It hits the second something hurts as it stretches or goes deep, the border of what some call *extreme sex*, and sometimes it's too much, too rough, a sign of pain, a sign to slow down. Anal sex is not a competition for how hard I can go or how much I can take — it's just a push against the mind resisting, the muscles tensing, buckling up through the primal desire to surrender. It's a competition between pleasure and pain, tension and release. That yelp was the sound of someone turning one direction or the other.

I was mesmerized and watched until the session ended — the bottom pulled off, needing a break. The top turned and looked at me.

We could have been an orgiastic moment there with all the onlookers, but I wasn't ready for that, so I turned around and kept going. Several guys asked me to go home with them, which I thought was almost sacrilegious.

Isn't this our church, here?

A couple of hours clicked by and the drugs were beginning to wear off. People started leaving. Parties die so quickly. I realized I arrived too late. On my way to the front, I saw the god top standing in a corner.

"I was looking for you," he said.

+ + +

He asked me to go back to his place. I rarely went home with people from events like this, but I needed something to do, and San Francisco gets shockingly quiet after midnight, after heavier, harder indoor plans are already set. We took a car to his apartment — he was, somewhat surprisingly, local — and on the way there, we talked about what we were each into. He wasn't especially talkative, but I shared that I was really into DP. He said *that's so hot.*

At his place, he told me to get in a leather armchair on my knees, ass up. "Don't move," he said. He put a blindfold around my eyes. Then I felt something, a toy, slick and round, pushing at my ass. He pushed a little eagerly and I pulled away. He slapped my butt hard, told me to breathe, and promised to go slow. After it was in, he said, "Okay, get ready." Then I felt the tip of his dick pushing in over it. I loved DP, but this was ridiculous. I started to pull away and he grabbed me by the throat. "No, *boy*. Remember what I said. Don't move. Take a deep breath."

I did, and in one hard push, he shoved his dick in over the toy. "Take the pain," he said. "Get used to it." I started counting to ten, a trick I often did when getting fucked to relax myself and slow my breathing, and by number eight, something strange happened in my body.

Take the pain.

My hole just opened — big — and he fucked me. I felt the toy stretching and his thrust sliding in over it and it felt wide and good, nearly breaking, and I realized I was on that border, moments from a yelp, but I was already turning in the direction I wanted to go. I've never fully figured out the secret mixture of that headspace or why the body clicks into place some nights and other nights it does not, but I remember dazzling myself with how easily I took it and just wanted more. I didn't know then how strong a hole could be or how much it could take, and mine was showing off.

He pulled the toy out and started slowly sliding his fingers in until all five were at the knuckle. He put a bottle of poppers under my nose and told me to *inhale*. I knew to count for ten to twelve seconds, hold my breath, then exhale. When I did, my body went putty-like, my head throbbed. I was warm.

He pushed his hand in to the wrist.

I felt a strange suction, the intense full feeling.

Holy god.

He didn't know I had been watching fisting porn on the Internet for years. He had no clue how many times I'd asked men online to show me how, or how many nights I'd tried to arrange first-time sessions that never materialized. I gave no indication to him that I was even into the idea of fisting. But he knew.

"You're taking my entire hand," he said. "Reach back and feel it."

I reached back, felt my ass, and the thing coming out of my hole was his wrist.

"What do you say, boy?"

I barely squeaked out, "Thank you, sir."

Thank you, Sir.

As glorious as the moment was, it was still my first full hand, and he couldn't do much besides get it in and hold it. He might have pulled his hand out once or twice and pushed it in again before I started to struggle and get restless and he said, "You're tired."

I am empty.

He took the blindfold off. Sunlight was coming in through the window. He helped me up, wiped away the gobs of lube on my butt and balls, and drove me to where I was staying — a friend's place just off the Castro. I never told him he was my first fist and he never asked. We didn't exchange numbers or stay in touch, but I found his profile on Facebook a few years later and he looked sadly different. He had developed a severe meth problem.

'Sup? PnP? FF? Fuck yeh.

I was sore for the remainder of the trip, which didn't stop me from playing the following nights, but it tempered them. The actual Folsom Street Fair — the main event — came as an afterthought, and by the time I walked through the half-million attendees, I was a ghost. The fair was great, but I found a man I knew from L.A. wearing head-to-toe leather and hugged him, and when I rested my head on his shoulder, he understood. "Oh, no," he said sweetly. "It's time for puppy to sleep."

Every pilgrimage to Folsom holds a lesson, and that year I learned what it feels like to go too hard.

That night, when every pig in the city was playing, I was curled on my friend's sofa, asleep. What comes back to me now when I think about most of my sexual adventures and discoveries are not the intensities or boundaries crossed, but the rests, the points of warmth, the feeling of a blanket after a breeding, morning light after a fist.

That's my San Francisco. The Golden City. The City of Brotherly Love.

L.A.

After my troubled San Francisco journeys, I retreated back to Savannah, which was becoming a place to go between places, a rest stop on my search for home. When an opportunity came to move to L.A., I knew I had to take it, and try California one more time.

The opportunity was with a national gay magazine, which felt like my destiny as a Queer writer. When I walked into the office on my first day, I looked like a Baptist youth pastor. I wore a dress shirt, khaki pants, and a gray wool blazer. The gentleman in the cubicle next to me said, "My dear, you look very nice, but this is L.A. You never have to wear a collared shirt again."

As happy as I was about the chance to work for a real publication, it was an unpaid internship, so money would be scarce. I decided to start meeting guys again.

I never said the word *escort* and certainly didn't say *sex worker*, but I'd been earning extra cash this way for years. I started in my freshman year of college, two years before I was legally old enough to drink. An older man messaged me on an app and said he would pay me for my time, which meant fucking in his van. It seemed like a logical, sensible trade, and I enjoyed talking to him after. Little exchanges like this happened throughout college, but I never once considered it a real job like my friends' jobs — as barbacks and waiters, busboys and pedicab drivers. Doing this was, in my mind, too easy to be a job, with too few rules. I could do it whenever I wanted, whenever I needed extra money. I liked it.

I like it.

My parents were wealthy and regularly reloaded my debit card, but it had limits — Mom could see everything I bought. Buying porn, toys, tattoos, or liquor was out of the question. This was how I paid for what I wanted.

In Los Angeles, everyone was more beautiful than I was, and I doubted that anyone would pay me for company. But they did. I had joined a website, Rentboy.com, which allowed me to meet and vet clients online, just a few months before I drove to L.A. The site's cheeky tagline on T-shirts was *Fuck the Rich*, and I did. On my first day at the magazine, the big story from the weekend, quite coincidentally, was about the site: its Manhattan offices had been raided by federal agents.

Professional pigs.

I was scared and furious and offered to cover the protests of the raid from West Hollywood, which were organized by local sex workers. I stood in a park filled with people carrying signs. These folks were beautiful, and of so many kinds, all body shapes and skin colors present, and the feeling among them was warmth and understanding. They were nothing like my idea of *prostitutes, hookers, hustlers.*

Dancers. Mothers.

These were people remarkably like me, young and awkward. When I interviewed people, I introduced myself as a journalist, but after the protests, I wished I had acknowledged myself as one of them. In my first draft of the article, I included the fact that I was directly impacted by the Rentboy raid. The site had been shut down for good.

But I'm here to be a journalist.

Writing was my dream, and I feared my side hustle would blow away my chances of landing a real job at the magazine. So, I chose to keep those two selves separate and rewrote the piece simply as news. I was just an observer. The article felt dishonest, and it flew in the face of journalistic neutrality, but this was my big break, and I didn't want to fuck it up.

As I learned the ropes of a busy editorial office, I also improved in the business of intimacy. L.A. was a strange city to learn in. It was America on steroids: glamorous, dirty, a city fed and fueled by trends. Smoothie bars had just swept through, spurred on by celebrity health habits, and people flocked to them like they were cocaine dispensaries. A client took me to the Beverly Wilshire where a collection of red Ferraris was parked by the entrance, but everyone inside wore flip-flops. Nobody cared about anything except being in L.A. The city was the end of some maniacal dream, a strip mall that exploded and morphed into hamlets and highways but kept its distinct sheen of commerciality.

I didn't belong there, but nobody did, unless they were famous.

Even with all the fucking and writing, I mostly just remember the clothes. Men could wear whatever they wanted, so long as they looked fantastic. The problem was, I didn't know how to look fantastic. I was too gamey and cornfed, too Southern. I wanted to be chic.

Some guys wore skirts, others threw on hot leather jackets on the streets of West Hollywood. Some men wore fabulous jewelry and piercings. I wanted to be like them, but everything I tried looked ridiculous and wrong on my body, my thick legs and long torso. I wanted to be like L.A., and more importantly, I wanted to feel like L.A. I imagined it was the feeling of being discovered.

Why can't I be a product, desired and consumed?

According to local gay men, I didn't even know how to walk properly. I stomped and huffed along, slightly hunched. A sassy queen taught me to improve my posture, how to walk *like a model* with my back straight and my chest up. I thought this a dangerous thing to do and worried I would miss something at my feet and fall. I've always been a ground-watcher and have never mastered the art of walking while looking up, as if the world was always a bit too much.

A gay therapist who enjoyed fingering me said my habits — ground-watching, evasive eye contact — were associated with Asperger's syndrome. I decided not to meet him again.

At the editorial office, my neighbor — the one who instructed me against collared shirts — was Harry, the art director, and we became friends because of Cheerios. Every morning for breakfast, I brought a plastic bag filled with dry Cheerios cereal, and on my third day I spilled them all over the floor and was picking them up one by one out of the carpeting when he walked in.

"Hello dear. What are you doing?" he asked.

"I spilled my Cheerios."

I am a child.

"Oh, you poor thing."

He handed me a twenty-dollar bill and told me to go get breakfast. I went to a nearby coffee shop and brought him back a Kouign-Amann pastry. Later that day, he said it was the best thing he ever ate. "There must've been like six eggs in that thing! It was positively sinful."

Most days, we got lunch together. He took me to a cafe nearby, and in our wonderful talks, we learned that we both loved smut. He had worked in the L.A. porn industry behind the camera, doing *all sorts of illegal stuff* during the 80s. And strangely, he and I looked similar, like we could have been related. Because I'm adopted, I wondered — as I have with every older man I've loved — if Harry was him, the lost father. Harry had silver hair and I was 22, but we both saw it.

"We kind of have that Keanu Reeves thing going on," he said. "We don't have that super square Hollywood jaw, and we have to do what we can to work around that."

I said I didn't know any tricks to do that. "That's a giant load of crap," he said.

We talked about him being sober for 20 years, about his journey into alcoholism and his journey out of it. We talked about everything — about who I wanted to be, what I wanted to do with my life, and he told me how to do it. He understood me.

At the magazine, I was nervous about voicing my opinion or pitching controversial stories, and he said to *stop worrying*. "My dear, if you want to write about sex, you need to write about sex," he said. "You're writing for free, darling. We're not paying you, at least not now. So, either way, the magazine gets free content. And the worst thing they can do is say no."

We talked about the past — about what L.A. used to be like — and I told him that I've never learned how to cruise for sex directly on the street. My evasive eye contact was a problem in a game where desire often had to be conveyed through gaze. "Okay," he said, "Before you leave, I'm going to teach you how to properly cruise."

It is a lost art, and I am an artist.

I told him I wanted to delete the apps and chase sex *the old-fashioned way*. He said that sounded *like a great idea for a story*, and he encouraged me to pitch a piece about the experiment — forty days in the desert without Grindr — and to my surprise, the article was accepted and became a hit. It was the most popular article on the site for a few days, so the editors asked me to pitch more stories. The comments on those early sex pieces were brutal and shaming, and Harry helped me through that, too.

"Writing about sex is always going to rile people up, and that's really what you want it to do," he said. "You have a bad reputation to uphold. I think it's better to start as a reprobate and work your way up."

+ + +

One night, an ex-porn star with a ten-inch dick invited me to his apartment in West Hollywood. He said some other guys would be there and asked me if that was *okay*. I said it was *fine*. The apartment was dark — the only light came from the muted television, flashing icily across the room, illuminating hungry faces and sweating bodies. The ex-porn star, who I recognized from his videos, produced a tiny glass pipe with a ball at the end and told me to smoke it. I didn't know what it was, and I apparently did it wrong. When I tried again, I reached out to grab it. "Don't fucking touch that or you'll burn yourself," he said.

He held a lighter under the ball and whatever was inside it bubbled, and the ball filled with a little cloud. He told me to *inhale*.

You blow clouds, bud?

The feeling was like life turned on.

Whatever this shit is, it's now my favorite.

He called it Tina, but I didn't know what that was. I didn't know anything about methamphetamine, and I didn't know Tina was a street name for meth. It was offered, just there. I'd done plenty of drugs over the years — marijuana, MDMA, bumps of coke in bathroom stalls — and they were all just okay, never anything amazing, never something I needed. Art school was the lovely land of psychedelics and liquor.

Now this.

The apartment was elegant, filled with modern furniture and featuring an all-white kitchen, and the men were absolute gods — chiseled, gorgeous, L.A. beautiful. I assumed I was not allowed to touch them. Then the drug really hit.

Hey, let's try this on him, I heard one of the guys say. He was pulling my legs back. A sock was stuffed in my mouth and a toy was inside me.

Fuck yeah, stretch him out. He's hungry for it. I don't really remember the sex until the ex-porn star crawled on me and said, "I'm about to go hard." I mostly just remember being splashed with his sweat.

Alex, apologize to your mother!

I was both aware and unaware. I don't even remember how I got home. This was not the murky daze of alcohol. It was better.

The comedown was brutal. I got very sick, and that was when I walked into an L.A. clinic and restarted my HIV medication. When the gay health provider explained that I was *decidedly wrong* about everything regarding my HIV, I pushed back. He said, "Girl, I get it. I've heard these theories over and over. No one likes pharmaceutical companies, and it sucks that the meds are expensive, and you have to take them every day. It's the same thing with cancer drugs. We are a market, profitable if unwanted. But if you don't take the meds, you'll die."

I'll die.

He had curly hair and a sweet round face with freckles. I've never been able to tell him, whoever he was, that he saved my life.

A few weeks later, when I was fully recovered, I messaged the ex-porn star again. When he grew tired of me, I found others, learned what to ask for, learned what *partying* meant. It never became unstable — I never lost a day at the office or showed up late, out of focus — but the comedowns were not pleasant and at some point, I wondered if this was something I should be concerned about. I was jacking off in bed and thought about my last wild night in a stranger's apartment, and I started trembling.

I brought up the subject with Harry at lunch.

"Yeah, my partner went through all that," he said.

"Really?"

"Yeah. And I had to tell him I was okay with it. I'm sober, but that's *my* journey, you know? I had to let him have his. I told him, if you want to explore it, go explore it. And he did, and it caused problems, and we got through them. You really can't keep someone from doing what they have to do, and I generally think it's a bad idea to try."

He was driving me home from work. We were somewhere in Hollywood. When he stopped at a red light, he looked at me and his face was incredibly sad. "You really have to accept that they might die. A person can die. Sometimes that happens when we're exploring ourselves." His were the same words from my father, from that clinic. *You'll die.*

+ + +

I started my personal rebranding with earrings because that seemed like the L.A. thing to do. Wearing them was a small act of defiance. Growing up in the South taught me things about having a cock — it meant hitting first and hard in a fight, doing outdoor labor, and not being soft. Girls wore jewelry and guys threw rocks at things, or whatever.

Whatever.

At first, I thought I was just defying Dad; later, I realized I was defying an ethos. I wanted to wear feminine things. The farm was far away, and I pictured L.A. like the opposition in a fight against the South and wondered which side would win. Georgia had guns but L.A. had influence. The country boys could hit the WeHo gays harder, but the well-connected faggots could spin the narrative and make the South and its citizens look like bumpkins and hicks.

Fight fire with fierce.

My idea of masculinity was born watching boys in my class and on my varsity football team. But more than them, it was the hunters, men who kept their crossbows in the beds of their pickup trucks, men who smelled of dried mud and sweat and diesel. I was masculine because of them — because I loved them and was raised by them, and because I was enamored with them and have been all my life. I know what the insides of their trucks smell like, what their necks smell like, what their John Deere hats smell like. I have wanted them since before I knew what wanting was.

All these notions of masculinity and femininity were brewing around in me and being challenged daily by life in a shiny, forward-moving city. I took on the work of unlearning them. I don't know if all this was related to my dark discovery of drugs in La La Land, but I imagine it was.

A guy in Silver Lake liked getting me high, putting me in lacy panties, sliding huge toys up my butt — I say *huge* because at the time they seemed big, but I suppose they'd look cute now — and calling my hole a pussy. One day he made me beg for it. "Say please," he said.

"Please fuck me."

"Fuck your what?"

The word was hard to say. I felt embarrassed.

"Pussy," I said quietly. It slipped out like the first breath of a prayer.

Alexander Cheves

+ + +

When the internship ended, there was no job. All my coworkers loved my work, but they just didn't have any openings or the budget to take on another staff writer. I would continue writing freelance, but that wasn't enough to stay in the city. Escorting was going well, but I was couch-hopping, migrating from spare room to spare sofa across the city — I even lived with Harry for a bit — and I knew that if I stayed, I'd need to land somewhere, make a commitment, and that meant finding an apartment and a job. More than that, it meant a decision to stay, to put down roots. On one of our drives, I asked Harry if he'd ever wanted to live somewhere else.

"Never," he said. "This is my home."

I had no idea what that felt like. "What's the thing you like the least about it?"

He thought about it and said, "I've never lived in a place where your intelligence counts for so little."

A week later, I was gone.

I missed my ex-boyfriend Miguel in Savannah and I hoped he would take me back, so that's where I went. Again.

I wasn't defeated by Los Angeles — in many ways, I was made there. Leaving wasn't a desperate act, just an adult one. The city was filled with idle days, hours to waste with drugs and wonder. The sunny hopelessness of Los Angeles was alluring, a treat to get lost in, a feeling easily stereotyped and widely written-about — and it's all real, and I enjoyed having some myths about the entertainment capital confirmed. I sat near famous faces and fucked famous porn stars. More importantly, I made friends — a sex therapist, talented writers, escorts, guides — and they said

I could become something important if only I could stay somewhere and see it through. But I was a runaway fleeing to my next spare room. The beds of friends and lovers were not always the best, but they made no promises to be, and neither did I.

Pussy

I had no skills in high school varsity football, so the coach positioned me as a second-string nose guard, a mostly useless defensive position that is only employed when the team is winning. He explained, his hand on my shoulder, that the nose guard does only one thing: "Just go forward. That's it. Try to push over the guy in front of you," the coach said.

"What do I do after that?"

"Go after the guy with the *damn football!* What do you think this is, son?"

After two years, that's all I learned to do in sports. Go forward and try to hit someone. I was not large or strong but could occasionally get low enough to knock over the center at his shins. I had no upper-body strength, so if the guy was big, I had no chance of doing anything and simply tried not to die. Play after play, I ended up on my back, occasionally with men on top of me.

The things I'll do to get wrecked.

Being on the team was great. Sharing close quarters with guys my age — locker rooms, showers — taught me how I was supposed to talk, what words I was supposed to use. Everyone on the team suspected I was a faggot, but they all grew to respect me and even like me because I really took a beating and was always very enthusiastic about it. When I came out in my junior year, a guy from the team — a lineman who towered over me — walked up after lunch and said, "Hey, I heard you like guys."

"Who said that?"

"Dude, everybody knows you're gay."

"Oh."

"If anyone says anything about it, you tell me. I'll deal with them."

A lot of gay men seem to share a common experience of mostly having girls as friends, but that wasn't my case. I didn't really have any friends, and then I had football. After that, my closest friends were guys, and they were as close to me as they could be. Some of the girls in my class were vicious and I was too inept, too underdeveloped in my faggotry, to be vicious back.

I developed social skills later than my peers, and during my awkward teenage years, I excessively flirted with every girl I knew, so much so that it became inappropriate. My parents got some phone calls and had to sit down with me and explain I was not allowed *to go around kissing and touching girls.* I had so many crushes on girls. I was nervous and silly around them. When I started thinking about men, I was conflicted and couldn't understand why my thoughts about girls were kissy and romantic while my thoughts of men were brutal — rape fantasies, duct tape, bloodied lips.

Go harder.

I didn't have bullies, *per se,* but the kids who didn't like me used the easy default jabs that hit most gay boys: jokes about poop and taking it up the ass. *Alex wants a dick in his butt* and *Alex gonna give you a dirty dick.* Things like that. I didn't think these jokes were mean, just unimaginative. To combat them, I circulated a rumor that I was a total top and liked to fuck guys, which really messed everyone up. One day in the auditorium, my class was doing a run-through of our high school graduation ceremony when a guy in my class said, "Hey Cheves, what's this I hear about you wantin' to stick your dick up guys' butts?"

"Yeah. I'm a topper." No idea why I said *topper*. Nobody says *topper*.

"Whassat mean?" said a girl named Britney, smacking her chewing gum. "You don't get *fucked?*"

Another girl chimed in: "No, stupid. He *fucks*."

Britney: "Oh."

The guy in my class, looking uncomfortable: "Well, that's straight. Sort of."

Sort of.

Continuing his joke, he started doing pullups on the doorframe — I still don't know how he did this, how his fingers found enough grip — when a teacher walked in and asked him what he was doing.

"Alex makes me wanna be more of a man," he said.

My being an alleged top offered him the uncomfortable idea of possibly being fucked by me — certainly without his consent, as most straight men seem to think homos are natural rapists — and that made me feel powerful. Jokes shifted from me wanting a dick in my butt to my dick being dirty, but there was a new kind of fear in that comedy. When someone teased me, all I had to say was, "Hey man, I can't help it that you have a nice ass."

It was a little victory, but it was also a lie. Before I knew that double penetration was actually possible, I masturbated in the shower to fantasies of getting double-fucked by two guys — and always the *same* two guys — from my football team. Sex became more freely accessible in college, and I found that I actually did like topping certain people. But we had to have that special connection that made me want to fuck them, and if we didn't, I was a bottom. *Bottomer*. And that's really gay.

Sort of.

Now I'm an adult, and a good portion of my money each month comes through sex work. I write magazine columns about sex and answer sex questions on my blog. I also sell my body to serve others' needs.

Sometimes, I help sell dildos and other sex gear to the masses far outside major metropolitan centers. I hope to become a sex therapist someday. I am a sex worker, on the page and off. I work in sex. Sex, for me, is both vocation and avocation. It is my ethos, my faith.

When I work as an escort, most of my clients want to get fucked, so I'm not bad at topping. But I was born with big legs, large quads, and a nice butt. And I must say, objectively speaking, that I have a really beautiful butthole. It has been described by one client as *sushi-grade asshole*.

I'm cisgender, which means I identify with the gender I was assigned at birth — male, allegedly — but I'm proud of my hole. I shunned shame a long time ago and replaced it with pride of my hole. I've worked hard — trained, tested my limits — for the hole I have earned. When it's getting used hard, I tell my playmates to *call it a pussy*.

That's just my thing. A person has to spit the word, barely open the mouth, push forth a pout. The second syllable is a hiss, a grin. *Pussy*.

P u s s s s y. Maybe it's the edge of those sibilant *S's?* I'm gay. I spit. I pout. I hiss. I grin. *Alex's pussy*.

Sort of.

Pussy is hated by some women and celebrated by others. It's the word that every guy on the football team used when talking about girls at school, particularly the ones they wanted. The word can be said with love or venom, worship or degradation. A lot of American guys into fisting, like I am, often call our buttholes just holes or, preferably, pussies. Sometimes, when they are really used, exhausted and destroyed, we call them cunts. I have been *cunted*. It's a thing that some people do to other people who like extreme sex.

I consider a pussy to be any hole, front or back, that gets stretched, fucked, filled, wrecked, bred, flooded, pumped, pounded, punched, licked, loved, spread, spit on, and opened for pleasure and sport.

Pussy.

Being a pussy — having a pussy — is hard work. It can be brutal. To have one as a cisgender gay man is to transform the body through sex, to undertake body modification by sex. Not everybody wants that. I do. For me, it is a right and a rite. I work within the rituals I was born to inhabit.

My cock is okay. I think I'm as proud of it as any person with a penis can be, but it's certainly not my star feature. I think my hands are better than my cock. They're medium-sized, smooth, a little chubby around the palms and knuckles. They are great for fisting. They open and help create other men's pussies.

I think my mouth and my mind and my ability to communicate in bed are better features than my cock. I've always been critical of my body and have never quite forgiven it for not being beautiful when beauty really mattered. In high school, I was covered in acne and had to take an intense medication for it. The side effects were terrible, but it worked. My acne cleared up right before college. I was a late-bloomer and had no idea how to carry my body or talk to people; I knew nothing of the confidence that beautiful people seemed to effortlessly possess.

I went into my sex life shamelessly because it was a crutch. I relied on sex to hide the fact that I couldn't read sarcasm or understand jokes or communicate much without it. Sex became my language, my narrative. I had to trust it.

+ + +

I look at those living at the top in their palaces of beauty. They float overhead. I wonder what the world looks like from their eyes.

Sometimes they step down from Olympus and fuck me, hard. I have been fucked by beautiful people and hideous people, by men who only deigned to touch me because they were high and by men who will only touch me when they pay for it.

If a client tells me they want a brutal fucking and they want it to hurt, I tell them they should probably hire someone else. I can push a person's limits, but I do it gently and encouragingly. I listen and use the weight of my body and my mouth to make them feel safe. Everyone deserves to feel protected in sex, especially when they are hoping to earn their pussy and working to get it stretched. I fisted a recent client in Soho who told me I had the energy of a brother and I said I appreciated that. We are brothers, *pussy brothers*.

Like most of my clients, he was an older man, more than double my age, with thinning gray hair. His apartment was white and cream colors, cotton blankets and pale fringe, candles burning on a clean, empty table. The walls and decor were the color of an old ceramic sink, or maybe silk, and everything was warm and soft, and he really knew how to get fisted. When I punched his pussy, I watched his hole bloom, and the slick candy red of his rosebud was the only pop of color in the milky room. It was a design triumph. It was Alexander McQueen. It was pussy.

"Do you mind if I say *pussy?*" I asked him as I greased my forearm and slid it deeper, nearing my elbow.

"Oh, yes, oh please call it a pussy," he begged. A few seconds later, he looked up at me, his face and eyes red from poppers. He seemed to be nearly crying and pulled me close to him. I kissed him and he held my neck. I cradled this man, my grandfather from another life, who was here in New York City getting his pussy long before I was born.

He witnessed the great clubs and the Fire Island holy days and then watched nearly all his friends die. They died just because of who they were, just because of the sex natural for them. This man, who has known greater loss than I will ever know, who has likely fucked more people than I will ever fuck, and who — against all possible odds — survived to be here in my arms: *Does the world even notice such creatures?* I'm honored to serve them in our temples and rituals of pleasure.

Our encounter had moved into an extreme place and he was still in the moment, leaning his head back, gasping, getting his pussy stretched around the bones and ligaments and muscles of my hand and forearm. His body was forged by things I have not known and cannot know, by places and loves I cannot imagine. I moved my arm deeper in him, rocking him — forward, back, forward, back — and he said, "Oh, please fist my pussy. Please fist my pussy." His voice trailed off, he closed his eyes, and he became just a hole, completely free.

Sometimes it is important to be just a hole. There are straight men everywhere who want to be just a hole. Many powerful and wonderful women just want to be holes. There are people of all genders and no gender who just want to be holes. Everyone has holes and most of us have difficult histories with them, fears and shames attached to them. They are the most intimate parts of our bodies. We're told to cover them up, clean them, keep them closed, hide them, tend to them in private. Our holes are where we rub and thrust, cum and bleed and shit. We could not survive without our holes, not for a day. That's how important and wonderful they are. The truth is, life's most pleasurable moments happen when something is either entering or leaving the body: music, wine, cock, cum, art, piss, fist. All through one hole or another.

Reading happens through the holes in our eyes. Slut.

I have felt defeated by my hole on countless nights when I wanted to get cunted, but after douching for an hour to clean the shit out of my hole, I realized it just wasn't going to happen. On other nights, my hole has brought me to the physical limit of human pleasure, to that place in the body that feels like the soul. I collapse into myself, surrender to a higher power, and I am pussy. That can happen for anybody. Let it.

+ + +

One night at college, I was eating with a lesbian couple at IHOP and we started talking about pussies. One of them was a painting major and she drew a diagram of the vulva in black ink on a napkin. Pointing with her pen, she said, "This is the vulva. Most people think that the whole thing is the vagina."

"That is actually what I thought," I told her.

"No. Only *this* is the vagina. And this is where we pee. And *this*," she pressed the pen into the napkin, "this is the clitoris."

"I've heard of that!" I said. "The clitoris is more stimulating than the vagina." I felt like a contestant on a quiz show.

"Yes and no. Everyone is different. You can be pleased strictly from the vagina. But generally speaking, yes, the clitoris is where a shitload of nerve endings are." She pushed her lilac glasses up her nose. "You've never heard of flicking the bean?"

"I have no idea what that means."

"Well, we don't have time for that tonight."

I looked at the inky black pleasure-thing. It was drawn beautifully, softly shaded, a bug opening its wings. It opened gently, parted like petals.

It bloomed.

What I couldn't tell her was that I sometimes had thoughts about vulvas. But being gay nearly broke me, nearly broke my family. Gay had to be the end point, the finale to an epic tale. I was gay. That was it.

Sort of.

I no longer think a single word can contain a person, and I understand the frustration some gay men might feel when people my age say things like that. We resist the words our forebears gave power to. I revere that legacy, but I don't know how to describe what I actually am. I still don't know how to flirt with women; they still make me nervous. I participate in gay male culture, though my fantasies extend beyond it. And even while some might say I present as solidly masculine, I love being feminized when I'm fucked.

I don't think being feminized is bad. I'm a feminist; I believe women are unquestionably equal and powerful and must have inviolable agency of their own bodies and holes and lives. I do not think it radical to see half of humanity as equal in every way. But I do think being feminized is brutal and hurts, that it is exhilarating and dangerous and wildly pleasurable. Having a pussy — wanting a pussy — is risky.

Risky pussy.

At the Queer student support group at college, so many people seemed certain of what they were: "I'm Queer," one person said. Another: "I'm heterosexual but homoromantic." "I'm gay and poly." "I'm a lesbian!" "I'm bisexual." "I'm pansexual."

They all sounded so decisive, so proud. I just said I was gay.

What a pussy.

I still say gay. The word doesn't require much explanation. But it also traps me. Two years ago, I was selling gym memberships for a luxury gym in New York City and gave a tour to a young, intoxicating woman visiting from L.A. She had an edge, a low voice, a sharp sense of humor, and I asked what she did for a living.

"I direct porn," she said.

I told her I was a sex writer. "No, you are not!" she said.

To prove it, I showed her my writing and told her I also wrote content for a sex toy company. My other job, I explained, was to describe heads and holes and shafts, fetish and cum and body-shaking pleasures in myriad ways. Maybe someone reading this bought a butt plug I made them want. I will never know of the strangers' holes my words helped open.

Though she didn't seem very impressed, the woman from L.A. — *oh, difficult city* — continued talking to me. She was wearing a leather jacket and had dark brown hair with a braid on one side. She walked through the chic fitness rooms without asking questions — she had seen it all, and she had seen better. She didn't take the membership, but I wanted her to take my number. We stood in the lobby talking and she said, "Which magazines do you write for?"

"The gay ones."

Oh.

That instant, a line fell between us. She couldn't be interested in me and I couldn't be interested in her. She assumed I was gay, and I was proud of being gay, so I didn't want to correct her. She left, and I got fired a month later.

That was the day I realized I needed to reexamine my words. *Gay* was no longer doing the work I needed it to do. What would she think of me saying *pussy*? Even now, I see her as a spirit guide, watching what I do at night with the guys who punch out my pussy, who transform me into an ecstatic cunt. *You can do better,* she says. *Take it like a man.* I do.

Sort of.

In college, shortly after the IHOP vulva lesson, I bought my first sex toy at a novelty shop. It was a small black PVC butt plug. I managed to sit on it, and it was incredibly painful. I was not yet a real ... *bottomer*. I cleaned it off, threw it in a bag, and forgot about it until four years later when my boyfriend Miguel found it and wanted to use it on me.

"Absolutely not. It hurts."

He convinced me to *try it again*. We lubed the thing up until he could hardly hold it in his fingers, then I bent over the rickety bed. Miguel pushed it forward and I yelped *Stop!* We did this — forward, stop, forward, stop — for what felt like an hour, testing his patience and mine. It finally slid in. As I feared, it was miserably painful, and I told him to take it out slowly. He started tugging on the base of it — and something happened. I told him to *tug some more* without pulling it out. He obeyed.

"Keep doing that."

The tug, the gentle tug, was so wonderful and unexpected. When it finally slid out, I asked him to push it back in. He did. "Okay, pull it out again slowly." He did.

Again.

Again.

He gradually increased his speed until he was fucking me with it — pushing it in and pulling it out rapidly — and I was gaping, my pucker pummeled and, finally, my pussy open. This aggressive play is what some people call *pistoning* or fucking someone with a plug or rounded object to make them gape. A gape happens when an object (toy, cock, hand) gets pulled out of the ass quickly and the hole doesn't have time to close back up. That feeling — the pullout, the tug — is how I became a better bottom, how I eventually discovered fisting, how I moved on from Miguel into dark and agonizing pleasures.

Our entire sex life as a couple became this. He followed my direction until I loosened up and let him take over, and that's when he went fast. He started snorting and said "Oh my *god*. Oh my *god*," and after I was so open, he fucked me as roughly as I think he always wanted to, and to our shared astonishment, I wasn't in pain. Nothing hurt. Sex felt good for the first time in my life.

Pussy.

+ + +

Gaping — plug-fucking — is what the guy from L.A., the mean top in Silver Lake, was doing when he called my hole a pussy for the first time.

"Sorry, that's weird," I said.

"Well, it looks like one." He took a video on his phone and it was true. My hole was so stretched that its edges were swollen and puffed out a bit, like lips. I thought of the IHOP pleasure-thing.

He continued saying it and I was baptized, initiated, part of a congregation.

Pussy, the word, the idea, tastes so sweet on my tongue. It is forbidden and true. I understand that it confirms all the teasing and mockery from people in high school, but stripped of its ability to wound, the word becomes fearsome. Those kids might have thought me feminine and pushed their belittling notion of women — their own moms, sisters — onto me. But I think of Pussy Riot. My hole is rebellion. It is protest. It is performance. My hole is political. My hole is punk. It is intentionally offensive.

Fuck you.

Those kids from high school, now grown and burdened with PTA meetings and sex lives cooling like a vanilla cake forgotten in the kitchen, can look at me with horror; I hope they do. Sometimes I really wish they could see me in black panties getting punched out, just as I wish they could see me worshipping pussies on other people. Sex people like me huddle and crawl around this word, spitting it into each other, eating its fire with the flick of the tongue.

Pussy.

There's an underground BDSM club near Penn Station and one time I walked in and the ticketing guy said it wasn't a gay night. "This is a special BDSM party," he said. "Mostly straight people."

I told him *thank you* and walked out. On my way up the stairs, I ran into a well-known NYC leatherman. "Great to see you here!" he said. "This is *my* event!" I told him awkwardly that I was *actually leaving*.

"No! You should come in! Take a look around! It's cool! This is my party!" and on like this. He let me in the party for free and told me to *at least do a walk-through*. If I wasn't entertained, I could *leave with no hard feelings*.

In a communal play area, I found a person tied to a chair, legs spread, showing off a pretty, pink vulva. A guy with greased-back black hair and thick Jersey accent was slowly sliding his hand inside it, and it felt wrong to be there, watching this, until he said, "Take a look. She loves getting fisted."

Her head was back; she was gasping, held. I've seen that face many times.

I've made that face many times.

The meaty part of his hand disappeared inside her to the wrist, and it was one of the most beautiful things I've seen in my life. I wanted to do what he was doing, to make someone with a vulva feel what she was feeling. I wondered what word he used, and just before I walked away, he answered my question:

"You like my hand in your pussy?" he growled.

"Oh yes!" she gasped. "Oh my god, yes!"

I have pussy envy. Whisper it in the hallways, tell everyone:

Alex Cheves has a pussy.

Tell them because it's true.

Hotel

A church near my family's farm announced that it was taking a large group of local kids to the North Georgia mountains. My parents told me and my sister that we had to go. My sister and I were antisocial critters from a farm. We had never known cul-de-sacs or neighbors. It was sad that our parents had to supply us with friends, but someone had to do it.

I thought the trip was a fantastic idea. I loved Bible retreats. These were places where kids my age became very vulnerable and exposed. The meanest, most vapid teenagers would be seen weeping with their hands raised while a white, thirty-something adult at the front of the room played guitar and told everyone that god was present.

Something like this happened at Bible camp the year before. Everyone was told to write down the things they wanted forgiveness for on little pieces of paper and throw them into a large bonfire. The ceremony was beautiful, and after the songs and prayers, I kicked through the ashes, looking for confessions.

On this trip to the mountains, I knew I would be in close quarters with older boys from my school, and that alone would make it worth it. I hoped they would finally see how cool I was.

My sister Jo really struggled around girls her age. She walked at the back of groups and was painfully shy. We both lacked any degree of social sharpness. She was simply aware of it and seemed to accept it. I, on the other hand, tried to be funny.

I think our years in Africa were mostly responsible for this. We came back to the United States having missed some important slang terms and pop culture references, and this ignorance dogged us for a long time. When boys my age joked and teased, I didn't know how or when to laugh. My laugh came too loud, too late, and revealed a desperation to understand what was said.

When Mom and Dad dropped us off, I recognized the guys from my school. Most of them were in the grades above me. I saw them in the hall but had never spoken to any of them. On the bus, I tried impressing them with funny lines from TV shows and movies, and by the time we arrived in the mountains, they all thoroughly hated me.

The church leaders drove us to a cold mountain river where we went tubing. I don't know what this had to do with Jesus, but I watched his creations playing in the water: the older boys, their bodies wet and slick, roughhousing, pushing each other under water. They made it look easy to be one of them. They misbehaved like anarchic angels fighting over Gabriel's horn.

This is before I'd read Nietzsche. Before Kant or Kierkegaard, even before Whitman and Yeats.

I remember the hotel room, the green hill illuminated by the light from the parking lot, the highway outside the window, and the sound of cars going by — late traffic out of Atlanta. The entourage of young Christians had stopped at a cheap hotel on our way back home. No one cried or confessed anything on the trip — the whole thing was just a lazy river ride with some prayers thrown in.

What a waste.

I was randomly paired in bed with a guy some years older than me. I didn't know his name, but I knew he went to my school. I had never spoken to him. He had bright blue eyes, curly brown hair, and freckles.

In the middle of the night, he brushed his hand over my boxers. I was already awake, and I immediately became hard. He brushed his hand again and held it there for a moment, discovering that I liked this attention. The third time, he slipped his hand in and grabbed my dick. The gesture was neither tender nor violent, just intently curious — he seemed to be testing its hardness, wanting to know what it felt like. A few minutes later, he pulled my hand to him and slid my fingers inside the elastic of his boxers. I held my hand there, resting over his skin, then moved my fingers forward, downward, into the dark. I felt coarse, curly hair under my fingertips, and then I felt something warm and fleshy — and touched another boy's penis for the first time.

When our quiet fumbling was over, I panicked, faked a nightmare, and started talking out loud so he would think I'd done everything in my sleep. I repeated the only name I could think of — "Leo," the name of a guy from Bible camp the summer before — over and over. I'm not sure he bought this performance, but he at least played into it. He shook me awake and said I was talking in my sleep.

The next day, the older boys pointed at me and laughed from the back of the bus. After we were on the road, one of them, seemingly on a dare, came to my seat and said, "Hey ... can I rub you?" Then he ran back to his friends, giggling.

I assumed my bed partner told the guys I touched him in the middle of the night. I sat alone on the bus home, almost breaking, not saying a word.

I don't think there were three words in my head yet. I knew, perhaps, that I should suffer.

Later, I learned his name — he, my first cock, my first surge of lust, spark of love. He left the school not long after to attend a more expensive academy an hour away. I saw him only once again, many years later, when I was a junior in high school. My family attended a megachurch in Athens,

Georgia, and one day we were leaving the service when someone called Dad's name. Dad turned and spoke to a man he recognized.

The auditorium was dark. Christian pop blasted out of the speakers. I was looking the other way when Dad put his hand on my shoulder and said, "This is my son, Alex."

I turned and shook the man's hand. He did not look familiar to me. The man said, "You probably remember my son. He used to go to your school."

The father, the son ...

The son was standing behind him. I shook the son's hand, and as I did, I knew I had touched this hand before, and I was certain he knew it, too. I was touched without my consent but did not feel violated — I felt unlocked. In the years following his little touch under the sheets, he evolved in my mind into an icon. I could have knelt at his feet like Mary Magdalene, oiled them gently with my hair, my hands, my mouth.

I did not know then that I would become a happily promiscuous adult who willingly gets groped and grabbed without asking for it by strangers.

I would grow to love rough sex, but nothing about that first experience was rough. He guided my hand along the surface of the bed as if to say: *here, please touch me.*

What about the dick? People have asked for details. I don't know if it was big or small or nice, I never even looked at it. And these details don't matter because I had no comparison, no concept of *dick*. More than his dick, his body, his heat, stayed with me. His skin was incredibly warm — were all bodies like that? It was cock, heat, sweat. He was my furnace. Who knew people were like fires?

I rage, still.

After we touched each other, we moved our legs and torsos closer, slid beside each other, somehow got entangled, quietly, because other boys were sleeping in the bed next to us. We pushed each other over onto our sides and attempted to slide our dicks in each other, dryly and quietly. Of course, we failed, having no idea what we were doing.

I was glad my first time happened this way — with complicity and wonder. I would not know how to write about the experience until years later, in college, when I read the poem "The Gas Station" by C. K. Williams in Professor Arnold's class. The poem was about the poet's own first sexual experience, which also happened in a city. Cities have long had a way of awakening beasts.

We were in Times Square, a pimp found us, corralled us, led us somewhere,
down a dark street, another dark street, up dark stairs, dark hall, dark apartment ...

Complicity. Wonder. That's the best I could ask for. My body felt like a machine that had just performed its purpose, moved as it was meant to move. The way we touched without instruction and did what we thought we were meant to do, with no words passed between us — we were pure. We were all raw need. He didn't know me nor I him, and we didn't need to know each other.

... where his whore, his girl or his wife or his mother for all I know dragged
herself from her sleep,
propped herself on an elbow, gazed into the dark hall, and agreed, for
two dollars each, to take care of us.

Alexander Cheves

When I touched him again, shaking his hand in a church, people filed out around us, knowing nothing of what we shared. The handshake lasted a half-second, or however long handshakes last. Dad said goodbye to the man, the father of my first, and my family left. I never saw him again.

I'm sure my parents and sister walked out of the church fussing over where to go to lunch and I'm sure I played along, giving no sign that I was burning on the inside. For weeks and months after the handshake, I carried his fire inside me. It was the same ache that every person who's lived in the closet has felt, something deeper than longing, like being barely able to breathe. I felt ravenous, starving. I hunted for him every Sunday, scanned the crowd entering and leaving, and never found him. Not once.

... *the holy ghost.*

I know he became MVP of the football team at the school he moved to. When I looked him up on Facebook some years later, his stated political views were Republican. His pictures were the expected ones from a good Southern man — standing in a row with other men, holding guns and red cups. He made no indication that he once liked to touch guys, even if just as an experiment. I could have reached out, sent some message, but what would I say? The encounter meant everything to me and likely meant nothing to him.

And the truth is, he could have been replaced by anyone and I would still be what I am. What lingered in my body after him had nothing to do with him. Not really. But all the same, I was grateful. If he told the other guys I touched him in the night, I have long since forgiven him. Someone might have heard us and he needed to give them an explanation for his own protection. I don't think we were very quiet. I had done the same thing to Leo, the name I repeated in my fake dream.

Take care of us. Some of the words that come through me now seem to
stay, to hook in.

Leo was a hyperactive, toothy kid at Bible camp the year before. He liked to throw rocks and get in trouble. One day we confessed to each other that we had *gay phases*. He asked if he could touch my *wiener* and I said *okay*. We sat next to each other at the lunch table, and I whispered, *do it*. He grabbed it.

"*Jeez,*" he said, "it's like a hotdog!" He was being too loud.

"Shut up."

"No really, it's so *big*." Even louder.

"Leo, shut up. *Stop it*." I pushed his hand away.

The next day, during quiet time, when we were supposed to be reading, napping, or praying, Leo came to my bunk and said, "Hey, I wanna touch it!" and I told him *no*.

"But," I said, nervously. "I liked it."

"You *did?*" He seemed to think this was funny.

I nodded and told him to please go away and not tell anyone.

The next day, all the guys were throwing things and teasing each other, and Leo shouted at me in front of everyone, *YOU SAID YOU LIKED IT WHEN I TOUCHED YOUR WIENER!*

I acted angry and shocked. I called him a *faggot*. I told the other guys, "I'm not sure I want to come back to this camp next year," and they said, "Hey man, don't let Leo upset you like that. He's just being annoying."

Leo became a source of ridicule for the rest of the week. He stopped talking to everyone. We talked about him, teased him behind his back, and he never spoke to me again.

Alexander Cheves

My actions were cruel, but his were worse — he blabbed, and in the closet, blabbing could kill. He didn't realize what bad things could have happened to us, trapped at a Christian camp.

Maybe the right words were there all along. Complicity. Wonder.

I stopped counting my number of sex partners when I passed 100 during my junior year of college. The last time I was at Fire Island, a man stuck a needle in my dick — TriMix, or essentially injectable Viagra — and I was hard for hours. I fucked a sweet 26-year-old with tender blue eyes, freckles, and curly hair who looked like him, my first dick, my first love, but wasn't. This beautiful man was someone else, someone willing to be part of this world, someone who chose it.

We were just two men in a massive sex party. Other men stood around us doing drugs and watching, sticking needles of other types in their bodies.

The 26-year-old took two big hits of ketamine and rested his head against a red pillow. The lines and muscles of his neck and throat, leaning back, letting me cradle him, looked, in the dim light, like a sculpture. I felt his tight hole relax around my dick and I fucked him the way strangers are supposed to fuck — selfishly. This rite, this savage act, was something we both needed, and we were both there to get it.

Grace. Love.
Take care of us. Please.

Backroom

One year, during Atlanta Pride, a friend said, "Let's hunt for X." I didn't know if he meant the letter x or that X meant *ecstasy*. I simply followed his lead and started asking every adult who spoke to me for X, whatever that was, and learned that if a person does that enough, they're bound to be successful. A man with a salt-and-pepper beard had the cache — the mystery thing was a little pill between his fingers. It was only after I swallowed the whole thing that he said I should have only done half.

We were in a club called Opera, which was created from an elegant old theater with a slanted floor and large stage. I started to get very high and there was nothing I could do about it.

Baby, just let it roll.

That meant nothing to me. He pulled me through the crowd, and as he did this, the people transformed. They slowly became very tactile, very blurry, very touchable, and I understood that this was the feeling of being really fucked up.

I told the man, *This is a beautiful drug.* Did I tell him that or just think it? This was the first time I realized a drug could be beautiful.

The man, whatever his name was, took me in his car to the next club, which was darker, sexier — he called it *an after-hours club.* I was learning so many new words — and while we danced, I realized my truck was still parked somewhere near Opera. But now I was dancing with someone else — salt-and-pepper beard was gone. Then, I was talking to a friend, someone I had known a long time. Or at least that's how it felt.

I told him I had to go get my truck and he said I should stay and dance off the high.

"WHAT DO YOU MEAN!" I shouted over the music.

"YOU ARE HIGH AS FUCK!" he shouted back. "YOU HAVE TO DANCE IT OFF."

Okay.

I rubbed him and smelled him, but at some point, I realized I was chewing the inside of my cheek when I painfully pulled a ribbon of skin off with my teeth. My friend saw this, grabbed my face, looked at my eyes, and pulled me off the dance floor.

"LET'S TAKE A BREAK," he shouted.

We went past the bathroom. There was a hallway that led to a large room with black sofas and fluorescent lights on the ceiling. Guys sat and smoked. Some were passed out.

I stood in the corner, spinning in my body. "Just relax," he said. "You're okay. You'll be okay."

Some men passed us and went to the back wall — except it wasn't a wall, it was a heavy black curtain that hung from the ceiling to the floor. *What's back there?*

"Let's go check it out," he said. He went in and I lost sight of him forever.

I pulled back the curtain. When my eyes adjusted to the dark, I saw two guys fucking in the corner. But that wasn't possible. We were in a club. I had walked from a dance floor to here. But it was happening. I was high and this was real. I knew both to be true.

This was my first backroom, the first time I stumbled into one, curious and unbelieving. Other men stepped in through the curtain, the veil between that world and this one, and I stood there, recognizing, I think, that I had found something significant to me — not an exact place but a practice.

I watched the guys fucking in the dark in front of everyone. In my memory, later, they would appear to be dipped in tar, wet and black, naked, made of alabaster and marble. Their worshippers swarmed around them, watching, begging to be chosen, touched.

I turned around.

A muscular man stood in the opposite corner as if he was trying not to be seen. I could not see his face or any features clearly in the dark, but I was also high and those features, if I saw them, have been lost to me. I could discern his shape, his great bulk. As I looked at him, he unbuckled his belt — metallic *click* — and unzipped his pants. I watched his dick flop out.

I turned back to watch the guys fuck. It was too much.

This is too much.

Other people crowded that side of the room and I backed away from them, stepping closer to the man in the corner. He stood still, waiting for me to come up to him, and when I did, he said nothing, just nodded downward. He was stroking it, but it wasn't quite hard yet. I could not believe that I was doing this. Without saying a word, I dropped to my knees and put his dick in my mouth.

I've never been a big fan of oral sex and generally do not like sucking cock, but his was perfect. Whether that perfect was a quality of the cock or the ecstasy, I could not say, but I loved that it was not fully hard. I felt it growing bigger in my mouth. He took my chin, pulled my face up to look at him, and in a breathy growl: *Hey, it gets big.* I could tell. I knew. He pulled my chin up again: *You wanna get fucked?*

I gasped, nodded in wonder.

Yes.

Then a voice behind me: *Oh, there you are.*

Alexander Cheves

It was the salt-and-pepper beard. He was standing at the edge of the backroom, holding the curtain open, letting in the horrible light, which landed directly on me.

We're going.

Still on my knees, I said, "Now? I think I'm going to stay for a little bit."

"With him?"

"Yeah."

"Okay. Well, we're out."

He was angry, and I realized even in my furious high that I was being judged. He was literally looking down at me, and with the bright light on my face, I felt exposed. I was a very young gay man on his knees in front of a stranger after doing ecstasy for the first time. I felt embarrassed. I felt naughty.

The dude with his dick out said, "Hey buddy, we're just having fun."

"Excuse me, I'm not fucking talking to you," my drug friend said. "Alex, why don't you come with us?"

I didn't know what to do. The moment was ruined. "You know what, it's okay. Stay with this guy."

"No — wait."

I was high, but I realized I could not get back to my truck on my own. I had no ride and no understanding of the city. I didn't even know where I was. And my ass wasn't cleaned out — I couldn't stay here and get fucked by this mysterious man in the dark. Still on my knees, I told the man that I was *sorry*, and I think I even quietly said that *I really wanted to stay*, but these guys were my ride, so I had to go. I stood up and left.

I went home with my ride and his partner, and after we had sex, we laid together in bed, and for some reason, I recited the poem

"For a Coming Extinction" by W. S. Merwin and they agreed it was very powerful. We stared at the ceiling as I became clear-headed, and with every minute, I hated them more. Salt-and-pepper beard drove me back to my truck and said, "I hope I see you again." When he left, I blocked his number. I drove to my friend's place on Cheshire Bridge Road where I was crashing for the weekend and that's when the comedown hit. It was my first drug crash, and it was rough. What burned more was a feeling of having made the wrong choice.

An older man gave me drugs and, in doing so, made a claim over me, assumed I would go home with him, that I was *with* him.

For the rest of my life, I would hate and avoid people who tried to perform a reach — a gesture, physical, spoken, or otherwise communicated — that conveyed a sense of wanting me to belong to them. This had come up in my past relationships, but he made it clear to me. I thought I had an issue with the labels — *boyfriend, boy* — but my true issue was with possession, the impulse people had to assume that affection was inherently transactional, that I was willing and ready to pair off.

No. I do not consent.

+ + +

I would return to that backroom on busy nights over the next few years looking for that mystery man. And then I would find other backrooms in other cities, looking for him. He was tall and muscular and faceless, with a big dick and haunting voice, and I imagine he was in his thirties. I needed to find him. Later, I searched for him in San Francisco and Los Angeles, and of course, he became something that was no longer a man or missed opportunity or even a moment in time. He became a small god, morphed into the holy, prized leatherman, the icon of my gay dreams, standing in a corner with his dick out.

I've comforted myself with the idea that he's still out there — that he's waiting for me somewhere in Berlin or Amsterdam, hard and ready, or that I just missed him at The Hoist in London before it closed. Maybe he has gone for good and had his fun without me again: on the third floor of The Saint or at Mineshaft or even on Fire Island in the Ice Palace.

I have looked for him — so many of us have — and along the way, surrogates have stood in for him, men on dance floors, men online. He was the one we promised ourselves we would search for. He was all the Tom of Finland men at once. He was the man we lost, the one that got away. He was the god we saw fucking someone at the party, the one we wanted to go home with, the one that died of this or that, some common death among our greatest beauties: overdose, steroids, heart attack, AIDS, suicide.

Do you have a minute to talk about our lord and savior?

Whenever I grabbed someone's shoulders in a backroom, put my arms around them to brace myself while someone else fucked me from behind — in a room, a stairwell, or under the dock in Provincetown — I held him. It was always him. When I die, he'll be standing there, and I will kneel before him, the light shining on my face.

Bathhouse

Several friends thought I was dead.

As I drove back to Atlanta from a remote mountain weekend, the messages and missed calls came in. A text from my sister: *Alex did you go to Orlando?*

I could have.

Initial reports said 30 people were murdered, then 50. Finally, 49.

Forty-nine humans — Queer, brown, happy — were gone. Just gone. Most of them were gay men, most of them had darker skin, most of them were young. I imagined their last conversations, the sexual encounters they hoped would happen that night, the glances across the room, the feeling of being strong, emboldened by liquor, brave enough to say *hi* to the handsome man in the corner. If I knew anything, it was the politics of a bar, how they played out to a soundtrack of danceable hits. I imagined their last song was in Spanish — it was Latin night — and they were really growing confident in their step when the bullets came.

After Orlando, many gay men in my social circles claimed to know someone who was killed. I did not, but I wanted to. I wanted to tap into something personal from the event, which became a national, sensationalized news story. What did 49 bodies, dancing until dead, booze still in their bloodstreams, look like on the floor of a club?

Queer men my age seemed to treat the names like they were celebrities, and this was perhaps the only way my generation, raised on social media, could contextualize violence like this.

How many friends do we have in common?

When their faces were given to the public, I scanned the pictures carefully. Did anyone look familiar? What if one of them had fucked me somewhere, in some city? I had no way of knowing, no way to say goodbye.

I didn't know how to react. It felt like a sickening indoctrination into an antiquated concept of life as a faggot. This was something that happened in decades past, not now. I was a millennial; my generation was hope.

Why didn't you shield us from this?

More than anything, I felt naïve. Since I came out, my generation had experienced uninterrupted success: "Don't Ask, Don't Tell" struck down, same-sex marriage legalized, PrEP approved. I really believed there would be no more loss, that history worked on hinges — that there were points after which social battles were just won, settled, finished. I had no idea that time often looped back on itself, that fury and fear could reverse the world — violently — like a river suddenly changed course.

Was the world always this way?

+ + +

I was living in Atlanta, and I was new there. Moving to the city was a last-minute decision. In Savannah, I was stuck — Los Angeles and my relationship with Miguel were both painfully over. Atlanta was just the closest place to escape to.

I got a job selling sex toys for a local company and had been working there for a few months when 49 people were gunned down at the Pulse nightclub in Orlando, Florida — a place I could drive to in a matter of hours. The body count made it the bloodiest hate crime in United States history.

Over the following weeks, conservative pundits argued that it wasn't a hate crime at all but something else — anything else, anything to keep love and mercy away from pansies with brown skin. I told my editors at the magazine that I needed some time. I went to work. I did my day job. I went home.

Mostly.

My life happened in gay bars. Where else could I go? It could have been me. It could have been Atlanta. It could have been anywhere.

It could have been Miguel.

The Atlanta bar scene was good, and because I didn't know anyone, I went out almost every weekend to make friends and fuck. But for months after Orlando, I started going to the bathhouse. This was a safety decision as much as a sexual one. Practically speaking, it was harder to bring a semiautomatic weapon into a bathhouse. The check-in attendant spoke through a thick window made of safety glass and pressed a button to unlock the heavy steel door to let me in. I was impressed by the building's security.

Like most bathhouses, the place was open at all hours, and I was told that fucked-up guys regularly walked up in the night and banged on the window to be let in, so these safety measures were necessary. The building was like a fortress for faggotry.

Beyond the entrance was a maze of rooms and corridors, hot tubs and steam rooms, an indoor pool, and one blackout play area with a sling in the corner. The place smelled like chlorine and balls. Every Saturday, the sling was mine. I climbed in, put on a blindfold, and let men walking through do whatever they wanted to my body.

A man walks into a club ...

Getting used by strangers released me from emotions that were new — a new brand of loss and the feeling of being too young.

My highest load count in a single weekend was almost 49.

Removed from life — being a nameless cunt in the dark with only my thoughts to play with — I started thinking about my friend Ber. He was another anonymous cum dump like me. I wondered if he was grieving the same way.

Ber and I overlapped in Atlanta briefly. I moved to the city, and a week later, he left for New York. But we lived together that week. We gave each other a sweet taste of a relationship that meant nothing and could go nowhere — that was the deal. I imagined him somewhere in Manhattan, underground, his body in a sling, blindfolded, being shot into.

Reload.

He and I shared many kinks; we both loved anonymous sex and enjoyed the risk of getting sexually transmitted infections, and regularly got them. Like me, he was unwilling to forfeit his freedom for a relationship — and that, more than anything, made me want to date him.

+ + +

In the bathhouse, I was safe. I was home. My comfort hinged on my ability to drop in, drop out. I realized I had a crush on Ber. It was a non-possessive crush. I needed nothing from him. We were friends and I was always falling in love with my friends.

I carried my thoughts of him through the damp hallways, the endless loop of circuit music playing in every room. When I needed to rest, I napped on the rubbery mattress in my rented room, no bigger than a bathroom stall, and dreamed of him.

In Atlanta, I developed the side of me that thrived in anonymous sex, and in that process, Ber became a kind of mythical creature. I imagined what he must be doing in New York City and told myself I had to keep up.

Reload.

For men like us, anonymous sex was freedom. No one got hurt or had to reveal too much — not even a name, certainly not a story. Ber and I had the power to dial back the degree to which we needed things from others. We could reduce the sting of losses and absences, let others appear and disappear without missing them.

Reload.

+ + +

We let the holy multitude — bodies who passed over us, exploded into us — be an indiscriminate horde, and that horde was the relationship we chose.

What's love got to do with it?
What's love but a second-hand emotion?

Still, I felt a little romantic. Before Ber left Atlanta, I even brought up the idea of us dating and he shot it down because he was moving, and he didn't do long-distance. Neither did I. His refusal and the promise that this was a brief affair made our sex in those final days especially good.

Every Queer man I met in Atlanta seemed to be friends with Ber and missed him. They said, "You should have met this guy Ber who used to live here. You would have liked him."

I was tempted, in those moments, to say that I did know him, to make some kind of claim over him, something I would never forgive if done to me. So, I just said, "Yeah, I met him once."

I had a crush — one of those moony affections from the afterglow of sex, the thing that sparks wonder.

+ + +

Was I capable of love? My problem was not that love was inaccessible. I just struggled in its delivery. I did not consider this a failing. I simply chose to foster something in the place of love — a bad spirit, an uncontrolled impulse. I didn't know what it was, but it made me worry sometimes about my urges, made me wonder if the trappings of monogamy and commitment would someday need to be assumed, like exile, in order to survive. I wondered if people like me had to eventually take up the charade of convention or be lost for good.

I wondered if Ber felt this way. The end result of my sex drive appeared, if not bleak, then at least lonely. I saw my future in the bathhouse, in the wet rooms where men smoked meth and stared with dilated eyes into the sticky, cheaply tiled hall, waiting. I was becoming one of them, and I enjoyed them.

Were we capable of love?

Love, whatever it was, looked too transparently like some kind of delusion. I suspected it was a byproduct of human cooperation, brain chemicals evolved to foster altruism in a species that dominated the world primarily through violence. Love was a mental salve for real labor, real pain. Love was an opiate.

Love hurt. I felt it when I looked at the faces of people killed at Pulse. They were people I should have danced with, people I should have loved.

Who needs a heart when a heart can be broken?

I wondered if Ber gave a name to his urges — if he saw them as something that haunted him, if he personified his impulses into a force to be wary of, fearful that it might take control. I've always held my own strange mysticisms, and this was one of them.

The idea of my bad spirit allowed me to deflect some blame. I had cheated on every person I ever dated — Miguel included. I had never once had a successful monogamous relationship. I was not capable of sexual fidelity — and more than that, I considered fidelity a fiction, a cruel and unnatural cage in which animals meant to breed freely did not belong. When I broke hearts and hurt kind people, I could say the failing was not truly mine — it was just my bad spirit, just the beast in me.

I imagined Ber and I both knew people with bad spirits that emptied them, left them lost and alone. I had sex many times in Los Angeles with a man close to my age who was HIV-positive and unmedicated. His goal was to fuck somebody different every day and I think he usually did. He wanted every sexually transmitted infection possible and had eroticized his own ruin. His fetish was to die from sex.

Poetry is sex and death.

He frightened me because I thought his fantasy was hot. Everything about him was hot. I knew enough about Ber to know he would think so, too. Ber would fuck that guy.

The man in Los Angeles — whatever his name was, it didn't matter — was on a full-throttled dive into hedonism, and I was afraid to admit that I was jealous of him. I flirted with that same erotic descent, the idea of not caring and getting lost, consumed. I knew how easily I could slip into that place where broken people lived. On my wildest nights, I wondered if I was broken, too. In Atlanta, my drug-fueled sex weekends frightened me, not because I could have died, but because I could have stayed.

+ + +

I met Ber while I was still living in Savannah. He was visiting town, taking a weekend away from Atlanta with some friends. I ran into him at the only gay club in town, the one where my ex, Miguel, used to go-go dance on a box. All my great loves were found in places like this — bars, clubs, on my knees in a bathroom.

49 people.

On that rainy night, the place was almost empty. The only patrons were me and four out-of-towners. One of them was Ber — a circuit gay, a power fag, or at least that's how he presented himself. He was wearing a tank top and flat brim baseball cap turned backwards. He had a good gym membership without needing to say so.

I was immediately after him and he after me. We danced all night and got drunk. When the lights came on, I asked him to ditch his friends and follow me home. The house I lived in was a twenty-minute walk away, and halfway there, I said, "Hey, before we go further, I want to say that I'm HIV-positive and undetectable. And I'm not a big fan of condoms."

I tried to make the confession sound aloof, uncaring, but privately I feared he would bail.

But then he said *okay*, and *I don't like condoms either.*

We didn't need to say that we would breed each other.

I later learned that I was the first HIV-positive man he knowingly had bareback sex with. He was HIV-negative and taking PrEP — a pill that prevents HIV infection — but even with it, he had been serosorting, at least until that night. I don't know why he took that leap with me.

I asked him what kind of sex he was into.

"Regular stuff, you know. Butt stuff. Fucking. Versatile. I get into piss sometimes."

"Great. I have to pee so bad."

"You could even shit on me, if you wanted to."

That's when I knew I was with a contender — someone who possessed a wildness that rivaled mine.

Reload.

The building I lived in had no air-conditioning and this was summer in Savannah. The rooms were dusty, sweltering. We sweated feverishly. With the windows open, the sounds of cicadas came into the bedroom. We pissed on each other in my shower, and I watched his puppyish face — dark beard, thick eyebrows, big tongue — lap it off the floor of the tub.

I remember getting behind him, spitting on my dick, pushing it in his hairy hole, and feeling that it was full.

It's poop, Alex.

I asked him if he wanted me to stop. He said *no*.

"I kind of like it like that."

So, I fucked him dirty, and nothing about it was ugly. If this was the shit-smelling apartment Dad warned me about, I belonged in it.

At some point, I found the container of Crisco under my bed. And then I blacked out, so I have to trust his telling of everything that happened next. He slid his hand in me, and by the time we were finished, our bodies were greased and covered in cum and shit and the antique bed was broken. We cracked one of the support beams.

+ + +

When I lived in Atlanta, Ber was just a rare visitor. When he came down to see his family, he spent a night with me. I moved to New York City two years later, and there we reconnected as fuck buddies until we realized we were something else.

I have never fully adjusted to words like *boyfriend* or *partner*, but I've not found better words, and they were easier than explaining to others that we were simply in love, with each other and with our own freedoms, and we respected both loves equally.

Non-monogamy was easy for me because I was always a cheater — Ber just gave me permission not to lie.

Even in New York, I felt scared going out some nights. Orlando stayed a dark hum in the background. And when I did, Ber reminded me that we were not here to survive, but to live.

+ + +

All the bodies that ever touched mine collectively would measure to an immense weight. What a thing to weigh on the heart. All of them breathed, all felt and hurt. This has always been a strange thing to think about, and if asked, I would confess that I do not remember most of them. I have wondered often how many of them are dead.

Who needs a heart when a heart can be broken?

If I could pull them back to me, I would give each.one their personhood — sound out their name, clear and true, and tell them what a privilege it was to share what little time we had.

Over the years, I often wished I could present my first night with Ber to the people whose *god hates fags*. We were everything they hate and more majestic than anything they could ever comprehend. I would lay the images down in crystalline sequence: the moonlight on his back, the coppery shit on my cock. I've wished that I could reproduce his sounds, his groans and roars. Watching him in pleasure was the opposite of dying — and for that moment at least, he was mine and only mine.

You must understand, though, the touch of your hand
Makes my pulse react.

I loved my dirty boy.
Reload.

Heaven

The best gay parties happen wherever we congregate. It's not about the place but the moment. Some of my best moments happened at Paradisco, a placeless party that once brought men together on the rooftop of The Standard hotel in New York City, and has now probably died.

Paradisco drew a mixed crowd — Asian, Black, brown, white; older and younger, rich and regular. Everyone danced, watched, and were watched. The music was actually classic disco with some contemporary DJ flourishes thrown in. It all made me horny, inspired, sad, knowing it was designed to be brief, then gone.

Paradisco welcomed everyone: gender-fucking Queer men from Brooklyn wearing white dresses and pearls; rich Hell's Kitchen power gays in Balenciaga sneakers; punk lesbians; straight-girl besties; and basic bitches from lower Manhattan. *Ew*. At one moment, it seemed like most men in the room were sporting a single dangling earring of a copper spike or a George Michael cross. Then, something new.

A medium-sized disco ball hung over the black-tiled bar and a fully functioning hot tub was, against all reason, constructed in the middle of the room. From the second floor — an AstroTurf-covered rooftop deck — I saw the Hudson River glinting as if made of melted gold, the architecturally disappointing *Freedom Tower* or One World Trade Center, the silver buildings of Jersey City shimmering across the water, the lower tip of Manhattan steaming, coppery, brick and glass and everything at once. It was a sight so lovely that it made me glad to have lived long enough to see it.

But more than all these magnificent details that defined the space, I went there for the men. They were intimidating. The handsomest men in

New York City were there. More than handsome, they seemed virile, ready, self-possessed, riled by youth. They had arrived in the world at last.

I wanted Paradisco to still be around when life returned post-pandemic — whether that's HIV or COVID-19. The physical traits of the space made it nice, but other spaces would make it nice, too. I had to remind myself that it could live anywhere, could live forever. Still, I worried.

Wherever two or more are gathered in my name ...

The best parts of my life happened on the deck of The Blue Whale, at Paradisco, on the second floor of the New York Eagle (and the Atlanta Eagle and the D.C. Eagle and the L.A. Eagle and the S.F. Eagle). But before all these, I had to navigate my first gay bar, and it wasn't easy. I remember walking up to the entrance on Bay Street and Jefferson in Savannah and nervously opening the door. The anteroom was decorated in multicolored t-shirts nailed across the wall bearing the club's name and a sign that read *NO HOMOPHOBIA PERMITTED ON THIS PREMESIS*. Behind the glass counter stood a large man dressed like a woman.

"You wanna ticket, sweetie?"

"A ticket for what?"

"The drag show." His tone said, *Obviously*.

"Oh. Yeah."

He told me the price and I paid in cash. "Upstairs, sweetie."

The room was some kind of performance venue and it was packed. There was barely enough room to stand. I cowered against the back wall. The music was absurdly loud, and I started to feel a little disoriented — a drawback of having only one ear with which to process sound. The music was the swingy, jazzlike opening of a gameshow. Then the lights fell, the red curtain opened, and a thin figure in a royal blue dress slinked onstage as everyone clapped and cheered.

This person was not as grand or glittery as the kind ticket lady downstairs. The dress was a simple blue slip, the hair done in a simple French twist.

Blue Dress took the mic: *Fuck y'all doing here?!* This ignited another round of cheers. Then the Blue Dress shouted to the bartender for some *pussy juice!* which a bare-chested barback delivered a few seconds later on a tray, kneeling. The drink was a light-pink concoction in a clear plastic cup. Blue Dress drank it in one long gulp, then leaned into the mic, raised one eyebrow, and said, "I'm Chablis. But you motherfuckers can call me The Lady Chablis, Grand Empress of Savannah."

She nearly brought the house down with that.

She pointed out anyone in the crowd and spoke to them directly, dropping reads and ridicule upon them. I loved the show but was grateful she didn't see me. I didn't know that I was watching one of the most famous transgender club performers in history. I thought she was fouled-mouthed and funny but didn't know she was actually, truly that overused word, icon. The Lady Chablis died four years later.

+ + +

The house on Pearl Street in Atlanta was a doormat for every gay out-of-town visitor. At any hour, I would walk downstairs and find people I didn't know coming in from late-night parties: porn stars, DJs, people in leather, people making *papier-mâché* angel wings for a costume. We spoke in fluent fag and said things, like *papier-mâché*.

The house belonged to the gay couple I was living with — a DJ named Glow and his husband Steve. A month after I moved in, Glow started seeing a little pup, which is an affectionate term used by some gay men to describe a younger man they love and guide. This is a tradition among gay men — counseling the young through their coming-of-age with sex and providing support and an assumed de facto paternity. We were all lost boys.

The pup was my age and took the name Bulldog. I grew to care for him very deeply, like a brother, because we were both coming into ourselves. But unlike him, I didn't have a gay daddy. Glow and Steve tried their best to mentor me, but they could recognize when a young man wanted to live off-leash. Bulldog and I had stumbled unexpectedly into adulthood and both of us seemed surprised and delighted to find it was unlike anything we thought it would be. We were learning the prized gay commodities of youth and good looks. We carried these currencies and were learning how to trade them for what we wanted.

Steve was a sweet but aggressive power-top who was fidgety and nervous when he spoke. He talked with grins and eyerolls that weren't always clear in intent, as if he was trying to tell an inside joke that only he understood. He loved to gossip and had something to say about every homosexual in Atlanta. None of it was ever hurtful or condemning — he just liked talking about people and who they were fucking. Sexcapades captivated him, and he was proud and envious of his friends at the same time.

The first time I fooled around with Glow — a muscle bear covered in tattoos that looked like the wirings inside a computer — he got tired of fucking me and woke Steve up from a dead sleep.

Finish him off.

"Are you sure he won't mind us waking him up?"

"Oh *please*," Glow said. "Get ready."

Getting fucked by Steve could hurt. He screamed in my face, *FUCK YOU! FUCK YOU!* as he shot his load inside me, marking me as part of the pack.

And I was growing. In Atlanta, I met good people, friends who taught me about drugs and how to use them and where to hold my boundaries. Meth had chased me across the desert from Los Angeles, and for my first few months in Atlanta, I still enjoyed it enough to start worrying. As has always happened for me, the right men showed up, taught me harm-reduction and moderation, and by the time I left, I had a better handle on it.

I still didn't know what I was doing with my life, but I was getting better at it, whatever it was. Mostly, I just went out. Atlanta was a city to be gay in.

The city was small compared to the West Coast fantasies I had lived in, but it had an outsized gay population. The gay bars, because of their limited number, became something very different than what they were in San Francisco and L.A. Everyone went out on the weekends to see friends, not strangers.

Two years passed before my bad spirit rustled awake with the familiar itch to leave. One night, I came home from a party and Glow met me in the front yard. Something was wrong.

"I need you to come inside," he said. Then he grabbed me and started sobbing.

He pulled me to the front porch and said, "We just got back from Chicago. We went to the hospital to see what's going on with Steve."

Steve had been throwing up, but he said it was *a stomach bug, nothing serious.*

"He has stage-four esophageal cancer."

The next morning, I went to the hospital. Steve was complaining about everything, the bed, the food, and the fact that he had to cancel one of his fuck dates. The whole thing was a massive inconvenience for him. *FUCK YOU!*

Please don't die on me.

Glow was fussy and fretted about the room, and finally Bulldog had enough and told the men to go for a walk. When the door closed behind them, Bulldog sat quietly on the hospital bed next to me. He was an ICU nurse at another hospital in town and regularly cared for cancer patients.

"He's going to die," he said to me.

"I know."

"They have no idea."

"I know."

And then this beautiful boy — this man — fell on me, and I held him as the shoulder of my shirt grew wet. It was then, I think, that I understood, perhaps for the first time, what it meant to be part of this gay world. To be family. I didn't know what to do, as I had never held a man my age in my arms while he was crying in pain. I tried to comfort him. But all he needed was to be held, so I just rocked him gently and kissed the top of his head.

I was useless, really. Worse, I was moving on.

Everyone in the house watched Steve die slowly. A stent was put in his throat so he could eat food, but it didn't do much. I'd never seen cancer so closely. It was bizarre to see a healthy circuit queen grow thin and sallow, hunched, old-looking. More than his bodily transformation, cancer changed the people around us. Some friends grew afraid and distant, like we carried the pall of death, and they stopped talking to us.

Glow simmered and burned, hating all the *fake bitches* and *faux friend*s in town. As a family, we discovered, in the evening of Steve's life, a new circle of friends who appeared on the porch to help — who brought food and drove Steve to appointments and helped clean up around the house. These were faggots who had also lost loved ones.

I stayed quiet, but I knew what the fakers — the runners and betrayers — were doing because I was inherently a runner. But his was the first love story I would see through to its end, and it wasn't even mine.

As Steve deteriorated, he only wanted to go out. To pay for his piling medical bills, he started selling dance floor candy under the radar. He told Glow to continue his DJ career, to keep spinning and traveling to nearby cities. But in time, Steve grew bitter and volatile as he became unable to do the only things he cared about — dance, drink, and fuck. In his absence, the bars took on a somber tone. On Fridays, between drinks, people in town asked me, "How is he doing?" They didn't need to say who. I gave the cursory details, never spilling my heart.

A generation of men before me buried each other by the hundreds. How did they do it?

One was too much for me.

The only place where I could share my heartbreak was in the bathroom or in one of the dark corners with a stranger, and I did it without words. *FUCK YOU!*

Near the end, Steve didn't move from the living room chair. He stayed bundled up in blankets, sleeping. But one day while he was out getting a foot massage, Glow cornered me in the kitchen and said, "I know you're leaving."

"Yes."

"New York?"

"Yes."

I don't know who told him, but all my friends were his, too.

He gave me his blessing, accepted that this was what I needed to do, and made some little dig about how he preferred a house, not a shoebox. This was his way of saying, *I'll miss you, kiddo.* He opened the door of the coat closet and said, "Welcome to your new apartment!"

I was breaking his heart.

The doctor gave Steve twelve months. He lasted six.

I'd never seen a dead person before, and certainly not someone who I loved and had sex with, had long talks with. There was, of course, a typical funeral, but the real wake happened in a gay bar where everyone came to dance. That place, more than any chapel, was where Steve's life became *life*. I decided that when I died, I wanted everyone I knew to dance somewhere with the lights low, kiss each other, get beautifully high, cum down each other's throats. And then, let me go.

Do this in remembrance of me.

I asked Glow for forgiveness — I was abandoning him when he needed family most — and he said there was *nothing to forgive.* I didn't think that was true.

"But listen," he said. "If New York fails, and it could fail, I want you to come back here. Promise me."

Even at the end, he was trying to be a surrogate parent.

I promised him, though I wasn't sure I could keep it. I've never been one to come back.

+ + +

During the COVID-19 lockdown, I moved from the East Village in Manhattan to a neighborhood in Queens during the dead of winter. My new roommate, an ex-Broadway faggot, took me to a nearby gay bar that was struggling to hang on but kept serving drinks outside. Sometimes the temperature dropped below twenty degrees, but still we went, huddled under a heat lamp near the front door — indoor seating still banned in the city — while a waiter dressed in a heavy coat brought us hot toddies and cider.

We were all struggling to hold on.

It was better for us to be there than in our little apartment, because there were others with us, other gay men holding blankets around themselves, sitting at the little tables. We talked about the things gay men sit around talking about — sassing, reading, snarking — and I told them I was afraid for The Cock, my favorite gay bar in town.

"The Cock will make it through this," one of the guys said.

"You think so?"

"I think so."

We were trying to convince ourselves that it was true.

The Cock was the last down and dirty bar in New York City, the kind of place where I could get fucked by several men in one night. It had a dark sex basement, and in the back, naked dancers with erections that bounced as the men thrusted and moved. Their piss-slits bobbed at eye-level in the dim light, begging to be licked. The bar was regularly raided by Mayor Giuliani's thugs — cops — during his urban cleanup efforts of the 90s, but it was still alive. The Cock felt like something from a bygone era, when men cruised the city's parks and piers. Would COVID-19 be the thing that killed it?

The guy said, "I'm amazed I never saw you there."

"At The Cock?"

"Yeah. I used to go a lot."

I looked at him, scanning my memories, which were vague and blurry, colored more by light and smell than any hard details — the way good nights should be remembered — and nothing came up, no registry in which I could check his name. "Well, you probably fucked me," I said.

"Probably."

Our little battalion suffering the cold was joined by an off duty drag queen and her coterie of friends. She wore face, a smokey eye, and a thick-hooded coat and ski pants. With more people at the tables, our conversation about The Cock spilled into a larger debate about what New York City would be like when things returned to normal.

Everything's in Brooklyn now.

Manhattan is dead!

We nodded solemnly as if the fate of Queer culture was being decided by this small, ad-hoc council, our own Committee on the Future of Urban Faggotry.

"At least this bar will make it," the drag queen said. "The drinks are cheap."

+ + +

My friend Cadillac died on Halloween some years ago from testicular cancer. I suppose I am allowed to call him a friend, now that he's gone, but

I don't really know what he was. I just wanted to fuck him, and it never happened, so his is a strange kind of loss.

I met him when I was writing and directing porn for a gay sex toy company. He was the model we hired that week. We were shooting cock rings, which are a nightmare to light and capture on camera. He took boner pills and stayed hard for hours. He had an impressive dick and absolutely piercing blue eyes under large bushy eyebrows. His mustache and beard were coal-black, curly, and coarse. He had a distinctly Russian look.

We did not flirt on set. I'm proud to say I always maintained professional boundaries there. Others on my team did not; they used the job to sleep with models, and I thought that was gross — and it made the business look bad.

All my coworkers knew I was also a sex worker, and all the models were sex workers, so I went out of my way to make sure the environment was a safe and healthy place to be.

But every porn set has that one guy who touches too eagerly, jokes too aggressively. On our set, he was my nemesis. For the most part, everyone hated him, but he knew when and how to impress the boss, so he remained on the team.

Cadillac immediately recognized my nemesis for who he was and ignored his advances. Later, when the team reviewed the shoot in the boss's office, my nemesis said, "I don't think we should hire that model again. He was difficult."

I ran into Cadillac a few times after that. We were almost the same age, and we fucked in the same sexual circles. We were part of a common subculture, Queer men whose sexual identities largely formed in the age of PrEP and hookup apps, which together had become a kind of sexual renaissance for us. Our lives were marked by the fading stigma of bareback sex and the reducing panic within the American gay ethos, which put us in strange positions with our elders, men who were still alive and remembered the loss and horror of the plague years. It wasn't fair to them that we should have such fun.

The fear of HIV was still among us, embedded in our language and laws, and still dominated mainstream LGBTQ+ narratives. But between us, me and Cadillac, and other guys our age, sluttiness felt wrong in all the best ways and became right. Gay sex was free again.

I don't know Cadillac's inner life — I can just make these intimations from his age and his scene, which was, in many respects, my own. Cadillac and I formed our identities in this strange dichotomy, a place between an older gay mentality and a new one, and I've often wondered if we will be seen as the hinge generation between *gay* and *Queer*, the break between somewhat fixed gay identity and a less labeled, less discernable, more flexible one.

I would have loved to talk to him about all this, as I have talked with others about it, but that wasn't the relationship we had. We flirted briefly at parties and talked about hooking up but never followed through with these promises.

One night, I saw Cadillac on a dance floor at a warehouse party in D.C. While we were shout-talking to each other, we touched and danced a bit, and I shouted, "HEY, I JUST WANT TO GET THIS OUT OF THE WAY, I'M HIV-POSITIVE AND UNDETECTABLE."

SO FUCKING WHAT? and he put his forearms on my shoulders. He shook and twisted his body. He was wearing plastic pearls around his neck and had glittery midnight-blue makeup over his eyes. He blew kisses and danced and pouted and completely celebrated being in his body. I have rarely been able to do that, as I've never been fully confident in my own physicality. I've also never been a competent dancer, so he had to lead me. He tugged me along, and I watched him as I watch everyone who thrills me — like a dog through the bars of a cage, wanting to run but never quite knowing how to get through.

The little moment in the crowd passed when someone Cadillac recognized slipped through the sea of shirtless men. They hugged and he moved on from me, as I would have done.

I assumed our hookup would happen. He texted me: *I know you want my cock.* I did. Years later, I learned that he had worked at The Cock in New York City.

He texted me about fisting. He liked fisting beefy guys, and at the time I was on a long bulking phase and was pretty thick. *I want to put my hand in you so bad,* he texted me one night. Then he sent me a porn video of him fisting a big boy over a table.

Then he got cancer. I didn't message him once.

I watched his diagnosis and his journey play out on Facebook. He posted about his hospital visits, his test results, what the doctor said. I never sent even a short message. *Hey, I just want you to know I'm thinking about you and rooting for you.*

It would have taken a moment. A moment to write, a moment to send. Why did I abandon him?

He had closer friends. He didn't need me. A message from someone like me might even be taken as invasive, insulting, patronizing. Wouldn't it?

He had testicular cancer, and at first it seemed taken care of. But then he went back to the hospital because it returned and metastasized. He posted pictures from the back of a cab on the way there. He shared a snapshot from his hospital room, his bright eyes and boyish grin. Sometimes he was wearing chic pink sunglasses. He always had something funny or dramatic to write about, some kicky comment about the nurses or the doctor or even cancer itself. He was having fun with this.

Please don't die on me.

Over time, the photos changed. His bright eyes grew dimmer. His skin became papery and gray. I had watched this happen before with Steve, but I never believed Cadillac would die.

Steve was in his forties. Steve waited too long to see what was going on. Testicular cancer was more common, and I assumed that meant it was more easily taken care of. For Cadillac, cancer would be temporary, something he would beat, and we'd fuck when it was all over, because guys as young as us don't die.

This is different, somehow not like AIDS ravaging beautiful young men from another time.

His pictures remained great. He lost all of his hair, but he was still wearing a tiara and plastic chandelier earrings. He was in a hospital gown with an IV in his arm, wearing candy-pink pumps and draping a feather boa around his neck. He was surrounded by friends with his nails painted. On Facebook: *Cancer, you're a desperate bitch and I'm gonna BEAT YOU!*

Then he died.

In the posts and remembrances on Facebook, I saw we had more friends in common than I thought. We were, in fact, so close through others. But ours was a dance-floor love, a distinctly Queer kind of longing.

It was a passing thing, part of a web of small connections and little fires. What did it matter when one of them burnt out?

+ + +

It is a painful thing to get through, but now I'm here, and it's fabulous. It looks just like The Saint, the demolished East Village disco. I recognize the layout. Somehow, I have been here before. "Hills of Katmandu" by Tantra is playing. I walk through the downstairs bar — men in leather vests turn their heads as I pass — and I walk up a massive industrial ramp. I'm on a round dance floor. It's enormous. Overhead, the dome — the fabled dome, it arches over us like some small heaven, flashing with lights along the curved walls. The lights, the lights: they project from the mothership, an alien-looking hunk of machinery lifting on hydraulics from the middle of the room. I know there's a Spitz Space Station planetarium projector in the middle of it. And there's Cadillac, dancing toward me, sharp-eyed again, crystal blue. He comes up and kisses me on the cheek. I try to ask forgiveness for not texting, but the music is too loud. Then Steve appears, fresh from fucking his brains out on the third floor. We all do drugs and they hit perfectly, all at the right moment. Over the roar of the music, I hear a scathing read and turn to see a blue dress and French twist vanish into the crowd. We dance with our fathers, the uncles we should have known, the ones who should have guided us. And they kiss their lovers, the ones they lost. Everyone lost in the plague has found each other again. And we dance, the machine rising from the middle of the room, the lights falling. The planetarium comes to life, and in a moment, all I can see is stars. All around us, stars.

Submissive

When I was little, I asked friends at birthday parties to tie my hands behind my back with balloon ribbon. Sometimes they did it, and the sight of me struggling became a joke, something to laugh at. I loved it.

I did things like this all the time. My parents likely assumed my behavior was just the theatrics of a child who liked performing and getting attention. But for the stranger things I did — like tying up my stuffed animals and hanging them by the neck over the staircase — they consulted a child psychiatrist. I know this because I sat in beige offices talking to very nice adults for several years.

Now that I'm older, I can see that I displayed some behavioral patterns associated with adopted children — delayed potty-training, for example — and I know for certain that one professional told them I would not graduate from high school because I was fifty percent Deaf.

I proved that professional wrong.

To explain the rest, I think I was just kinky and didn't have the words for it yet. Take the balloon ribbon thing: years later, I learned this was part of a kink called bondage. I tied up all my toys because I saw Disney characters getting tied up and captured, and I didn't have the language to say how those scenes made me feel.

I felt something stirring when Leonardo DiCaprio was handcuffed in *Titanic*, when Chris O'Donnell was tied up and gagged with duct tape in *Batman Forever*. But my earliest trigger was when Captain John Smith in Disney's *Pocahontas* was captured and tied to a pole in a teepee. I imagined being in this scene for years after. I dreamed of finding Smith there, stepping around him, and seeing the rope around his wrists.

I continued having this dream for years and gradually placed other childhood crushes in Smith's place, tied to the same pole: Batman,

Spider-Man, and Chris O'Donnell, many times. I don't remember when the dream switched, when one of these superheroes found me tied to the pole, but I know they didn't save me. I did not want to be saved.

These feelings have been with me since well before puberty. They acquired me. I didn't acquire them. Kink has been my nature from my earliest days.

Now that I'm an adult with rent and therapists, I sometimes have to remind myself that I'm still a version of that boy on the playground wanting to be captured. It was so thrilling, being bound, even if the game was pretend. I know now that I'm more submissive than dominant, and words like these — *kinky, submissive, dominant* — are the kink community's attempt to codify me. I'm not sure these words always work, but I have no other words, so I use them.

These desires, captured by words and yet still beyond them, are sleeping in me even when I'm not doing kink. I have to remind myself of this, too. Kink — like homosexuality, like Queerness — is not performative. These words don't define the sex I like. They signal who I am.

Like most adults, I go through dry spells, and in them, I wonder if my hungers from childhood were just a dream. Then I remember how I went years knowing but never acting, never making the connection that having sex with my hands tied was something I actually wanted.

On the playground and at birthday parties — in slings and sex clubs — the little beast in me was real. Kink just gave it a name.

+ + +

Night in New York: I left a client's apartment and was walking to the train when a man messaged me on a fetish app and told me all of the things he wanted to do to me. He was visiting the city from Poland and was breathtakingly beautiful. He had a nice hotel room in the West Village.

But after some chatty exchanges, I realized we wanted different fantasies. He wanted a pain pig to kick around for the weekend. I admire guys who enjoy that, but that's not my kink. I just wanted a top who would ignore me when I said *no*.

I messaged the handsome Polish man and said we were not a match, and I had to pass on our imagined encounter. He sent back this message: *Then you're not a real submissive. You're just another fake.*

I'm HIV-positive, so I'm accustomed to people being nasty when they realize I'm not what they want. Rejection has stung me so many times that I don't feel it anymore — I can forget someone and my desire for them with one tap on my phone screen. But that night, his remark burned me.

His insult scratched around in my head and made me face up to something that had bothered me for years: other kinky people seemed more certain of all this, or at least more attached to the ritual of it, the names and terms they could live inside. When I went to large-scale kink events — to Folsom in San Francisco, International Mister Leather in Chicago, or Mid-Atlantic Leather in Washington, D.C. — I always felt like most of the people there were preoccupied with words like *submissive* and *boy* and *pup*. They seemed so clear in their kinks, so definite about what they wanted, so committed to their fantasies becoming real. I've always felt a step removed from them.

Am I just pretending, just a fake?

In college, I watched fisting porn for the first time while I was sitting in my car. I was parked outside of a tanning salon and it was raining. To put off the cold, wet run across the parking lot, I hunted for sex videos on my phone. I wasn't looking for fisting, but that's the glory of porn; I took a sudden stumble into things unknown, and soon a guy was standing behind a man who was bent over and showing off his beautiful hole. But, instead of fucking him, the guy shoved his entire forearm into the man's rectum, then pulled it out quickly. The bottom's rectal walls bubbled and bloomed out of his ass, the color of red velvet cupcakes. The top pushed the bubble back in. *That's my boy.* I would later learn this bright red bloom is called a rosebud.

Am I a good boy?

My gut reaction to the video was intense revulsion to the point of nearly being sick. What happened in it didn't seem real. The image replayed over and over in my mind while I was sizzling in one of the tanning beds, and I wondered if I had just watched a video of someone being permanently mutilated.

This is my body, broken for you.

I remembered the video description — the word *fisting* — and searched for fisting porn some weeks later. After a little research, I learned that rosebuds and hole prolapses are an intentional thing that some people like to do, but it's not something all fistees want. Some of the videos were hot, but fisting itself was not something I would ever partake in. I was just watching. I had no idea how much I would one day come to love it. I still get scared a little bit every time I want to ride a wrist.

I knew some of my kinks. I had words for them. They could be listed out: *bondage, sensory deprivation, submission*. Years would pass before I added *FF* to the list.

I eventually explored my dominant side. I found it powerful to cover someone's mouth, particularly when they were experiencing pain. I did that to others because I enjoyed it being done to me. The sounds I've made with duct tape over my mouth echoed deeply inside me.

As a top, I learned how to guide someone along that delicate line between pain and pleasure because, as a bottom, I liked to ride it. For me, like so many other kinky people, pushing that boundary — playing with it, extending it, stretching its margins — became a sacred language shared among those who took power and those who gave it up. For all my communication failures elsewhere, this tortured tongue was one I seemed to understand.

+ + +

In high school, I had a vorarephilia-cannibalism fantasy, one I've never fully let go. It's been alarming in the years since to have seen public figures shamed, investigated, and even sent to prison for having this little, niche twist I share with them. I don't get it: it's somehow okay to wrap tongues, bite lips, swap spit, suck cock, and swallow cum, but entertaining that these acts of voracious bodily consumption might become a literal devouring turns most people inside out. Don't get me started on the eucharist.

Cannibals. Vampires. Christians.

I've beat off to videos that look very much like rape (consensual non-consent, or "rape fantasy") and videos where someone was clearly in great pain. I thought these videos were beautiful, a great form of art, because they revealed new dimensions of the human sexual experience. I've seen fisting videos that shocked me, featuring holes that endured deeper and harder play than I will ever be able to do, holes that have graduated beyond the seemingly fixed limits of human anatomy and demand to be plugged with toys that defy the mind. The people of all genders who have trained and achieved this level of play and pleasure became my heroes.

Many people have told me that I am warped, that something is wrong with me. They have usually placed blame on some trauma or childhood abuse. While these painful experiences might have inspired — unleashed — fetishes for some, I've always found that explanation to be too easy. What if there is no *why* to kink? What if it just *is*, like an ear that doesn't work, or a butthole made to be wrecked? What if the little beasts inside got born with us, twins tucked away?

+ + +

You're just another fake.

My boyfriend Ber has remained one of the most impressive sexual creatures I've ever known. He evolved from a very socially withdrawn person who did not have sex once in college into what he was when I met him — a sex beast. Late-bloomers often try to make up for lost time and he has done so tenfold. But there have been many nights in our relationship when we've both felt like frauds. He and I have always enjoyed sex parties and have had many wild nights in crowds of strangers, but sometimes we've stayed in, paralyzed, doubting ourselves. We've been defeated, when our bodies wouldn't cooperate, or when we simply tired out. He and I could have gone to a party and played in the back but staying inside limited the risk that we would see our fantasies clash with an opposing concept — that maybe we were not the hedonic beasts we liked to think we were.

Every time I've walked into a dark room where people were fucking, I've felt overwhelmed. I have walked into rooms like that for a decade, but I still doubt my abilities every time. And that's why the Polish dom's words stung so much — because I didn't want to be considered a fake.

Every moment I've struggled — every time I've had to tell someone to slow down or use more lube, every time I've had to clean my cunt again in a public toilet — has threatened the dream I hold of myself as a small, uninhibited fuck god.

But then, the wonder! The times it worked, when my body unlocked and my fears gave way, reminded me that this thing, this animal, was doing what it needed to do. The dream was authenticated. I became real.

I could be something else, something other than *submissive*. I knew many submissive men with more kinks than I had, with fewer limits than I had. Did I measure up? I had been given a strange handful of terms — *submissive, faggot, gay* — but I could just as easily be understood by different names. When I started in kink, I was into *dog play*, a form of canine role-play that has since been curiously reformed into something called *pup* — a gentler, less sex-focused scene — and when I was a human dog with a human handler, I assumed the dog name *Beastly*.

I am tattooed with a beastly mark.

I eventually moved on from the need to bark and howl, wearing a canine-looking mask while getting hate-fucked, but the nickname stuck — friends and lovers still use it.

Alexander Cheves

The truth is, I started feeling trapped by *Beastly*, too — a name that often felt truer than the one printed on my driver's license. Was I just older, more advanced? Or was this the thing in me that hated being named? I have existed between selves, suspended in the act of becoming, discovering a new hunger.

You're not a real submissive.

Fine. That may have been true. But I wondered what I would be next.

June

Queer people were gathered in New York from across the globe for World Pride. They filled the park outside the historic Stonewall Inn, the site of the gay liberation riots in 1969. On that night fifty years ago, Black and brown transgender people set us on our path to freedom. We have made it here, now, because of them. With worldwide homos gathered, we spoke finally in one tongue: the language of the unhidden. We sat and strolled, danced and laughed in the sun.

I went to a rooftop party at a gay man's penthouse with a pool deck overlooking Chelsea. There, I got fucked in the bathroom over some potted flowers. The door to the bathroom wouldn't lock and a small crowd gathered to watch, my boyfriend included. After my little show, everyone laughed about it and someone brought out a plate of fried chicken.

Is this the victory of the last fifty years?

The faggots in my orbit treated the entire celebration like Pride amplified. Still a fuck fest, still a party, just on a global scale with global sexual contenders. New York was indeed selected by some international committee as the World Pride destination that year because of the Stonewall anniversary. Some marketing person successfully branded the whole ordeal #Stonewall50.

I hated the hashtag.

Later, I walked in the quiet hours through the city and was stunned. There were so many men in town. Every hotel in New York was filled with sodomy, flooded with semen.

But where were the others, the ones supposed to be here? We had arrived at their party. I felt like a sad stand-in, a weak representative of the prototypical gay man, having to be emblematic of a lost generation. I hoped the ghosts could see the celebrations through my eyes.

The last half-century for faggots was one marked by loss with rare moments of winning among the dying.

It's okay. I'm on PrEP!

At the end of the maddening month, Ber and I went to the Madonna concert on Pier 97. Thousands of shirtless homos were crammed onto a dense, claustrophobic strip of concrete sticking out into the Hudson River. Everyone I knew did bumps of ketamine and doses of GHB. I did, too. But in the sweet stupor of the crowd — pit sweat and cologne, a waft of poppers through the naked shoulders — I pictured us overhead and realized with horror that our only way out was the narrow space next to the stage, which was mostly blocking the exit. We were like fish in a barrel.

"What if someone wanted to kill us with a gun or a bomb?" I said to Ber. I was scared. This was the lesson of living in America. Know the exits.

"Babe, you just can't think about that. You just can't think about it."

I nodded. *Okay*.

"And besides," he said, "How else would you want to go?"

+ + +

The air is filled with flowers. At every subway station, a man in leather cruises me. We sneak off into sticky places, foul-smelling and underground. When the big weekend comes — the march, the parade — the city is bombed with confetti and color. Old men everywhere cheer. I have dinner with my daddies and their daddies. On my way back to my apartment, I pass bathhouses and gay bars, their electric signs sparking through the avenues in the dusk. Evenings in New York are why we live here. I dip through the Ramble and it's flooded with men who flood me.

In all our little watering holes, all ages, all children of progress, cheering, the delicate sound of glasses touching together over a table. Kisses from now to back then, connected and wet. Everyone meant to be here is here. Gleeful silver-haired couples toast the decades and the city burns with love. This is our trajectory. No one looks back. No one needs to, because no one has died. No one has been left behind. We all made it to their party.

+ + +

Instead, the crowd was young, or at least the part of it that I saw. Victories won by people in the past were celebrated all month by those who came after them or outlived them. We'd just shown up, really.

I didn't have the money to go to any of the big special conferences or speaker events, but I knew that some ACT UP folks did a talk, and Miss Major, a legendary transgender activist, gave a speech somewhere. I couldn't make it. I mostly sat out that month. I was a little triggered to over-use drugs, so I knew I had to step away a bit, and in that distance, I tried to see the revelry for what it was: the sex everyone was having, that my friends abandoned each other for, was its own kind of love letter to the past. People got fucked like our ancestors once did; people fucked in their honor. More than any law passed, it was our willingness to be these things, feisty and open, screwing on balconies and rooftops, that made us win. I can't say hedonism alone made the decades of death worth it, but it helped me know who and what I was — something owed to people I would never meet.

I was admittedly a downer for most of it.

I don't know why I could not let up. I think my mood was, partly, a self-moderation tactic, a way to avoid a messy binge, but it extended into my overall sense of self. Ber even asked why I positioned myself in the past and I had to tell him — or maybe I imagined I told him — that I did not, that I was just a writer who understood narrative. When I tested positive, I had to re-contextualize my life once I learned it had all been prologue to that first page, that first hour as something new. Mark Strand puts it best:

I am a new man.
I snarl at her and bark.
I romp with joy in the bookish dark.

And what a prologue! What a brutal, agonizing one! The story of AIDS was just relayed to me, just handed down. I did not live it. And even still, as a feeling human, it broke me. I could not think of anything worse than AIDS, anything more undeserved. Death from fucking. Death from desire. Death from love.

I had abandoned shame. I had abandoned AIDS, the idea, the myth, the narrative. It was not judgment or chastening. I just had a virus in my blood.

My god, why have you abandoned me?

World Pride in New York City was beautiful because of the people and because everyone seemed happy. The city was just so fucking gay. I wished it would last. I joked, in my meanness, that we should seize power over New York and form a gay city-state while we could. *God hates straights*, and all that.

Ber was right, of course. There was no other place I'd rather die than among my own. And anyway, it ended, and I was still a cocksucker snuggled up with him. After the posters peeled off the walls and fences and the streets were scrubbed of glitter, I was still a faggot lucky enough to live in such a place and time, to possess such a life — one from which I wanted little else than for there to be more of us, together.

Doubles

A few months into the COVID-19 lockdown, I took doubles — meaning two full fists of a grown man pushed inside my hole, my pussy, at the same time. Among my fellow fisting aficionados, this is considered a rather significant accomplishment. Fisting is not for the timid, and taking doubles is a badge of honor — a point of pride — in what can be a rather competitive brotherhood dedicated to this extreme sex act.

It's hard to think about it now because the experience was so wondrous and frightening. I wasn't quite ready for two large, meaty man hands inside my rectum, but he charged ahead and stretched me wider than I'd ever been before. I was nothing but open hole, pure pussy. He knew — could tell — I was ready for both and when it happened, I could feel myself giving way, collapsing into my own void and around his wrists, and then I was floating.

I was really fucked up, and even in my drugged stupor, I knew I was pushing the limit of injury. He was too rough, too fast, and I told him to slow down. I don't know if he didn't notice what I said or just ignored it, or if I was even cognizant enough to actually tell him that. Maybe I just told him to ease up in my memory.

Thankfully, I didn't get hurt, and after adjusting to the feeling of both his hands inside me, I admit that it felt magnificently good.

Getting your butthole stretched feels fantastic, but most people freak at the mention of fisting. I always wonder: what precise dilation of my hole is officially acceptable? A finger is fine, maybe two. Even straight guys love getting their prostates massaged during a spa visit or on their birthdays. A cock is acceptable, desirable, and the bigger the better for most people. But hit four fingers, collapse the thumb and push past the knuckle and suddenly I've dipped into a strange territory that many people consider extreme and dangerous. I wish I knew the allowable limit for butthole stretches, but I don't, so I just keep going. I've known men who have taken three fists. I've known men who have taken an entire foot. It's just the next stretch.

Breathe. Look at me. I said, breathe ...

After sobering up, I regretted the night. All of it. I wasn't a sober person, but I had a counselor who helped me keep my recreational drug use in check. I was one of her "low-risk" clients because I'd never been high for two days in a row, never lost a job, never come close to homelessness, never been hospitalized, never had any trouble maintaining friendships or relationships or work. I sought out her services myself — or, rather, the services of the agency I used, which matched me with her — because I respected drugs and everyone who enjoys them should have a supporter to help keep their enjoyment in check. Drugs are dangerous and fun. Like fisting.

I'm not a fan of cults or faith cures, so I've never been able to successfully align myself with 12-step programs, but I decided to be more proactive with my therapy when I moved to New York, the city of nightly wonders. For me, life in this sleepless city demanded a decent therapist.

The doubles were frightening, and maybe the fear I felt wasn't of the act itself but of a miscommunication, which can happen so easily, especially when drugs are involved. I won't say I felt violated or assaulted. If anything, I just felt reckless and something like shame, but not really. It was more like an amateur's embarrassment, or awkwardness, for having lost control of my own situation, not for my blown-out hole. My hole was shameless.

It was a familiar feeling, one regularly attached to my best nights. My cringy discomfort appeared everywhere and often, in any activity the cultures I inhabit defined as excessive or sick. In those moments, so many people have slipped into self-pathology and decided they're sex addicts or assume some other bullshit psycho-branding when they've wanted things that were, by most standards, extreme or unconventional.

But *extreme* and *unconventional* are the thrill. My hole has thrilled both me and the men who have played in it. Loving hole made none of us ill or evil. What we chose to do for our bodies was simply part of human sexual experience, part of hunting down the biggest pleasure possible, if not the most common among the countless options. Fisting has been around for centuries, as far as we can tell.

Push out. Now, surrender. I'm in ...

As beautiful and smooth as his hands were, as much as I loved the moment when they were both in me, palm to palm, as if in prayer, I decided I would not play with him again.

I did have regrets. I should not have gotten so fucked up in the middle of a pandemic. Other men I'll never remember moved through that small, dirty apartment, played inside me on a sticky bed wrapped in a black rubber waterproof sheet. The night could have been what public health experts called a *superspreader* event during the early months of the COVID-19 pandemic. I don't know how long he was playing before I got there or how many men had played with him before I arrived. I was irresponsible that night, but not because I took two fists up my butt.

The night comes back to me now in shades of blue and green, sea colors, the float through his apartment. Dirty dishes and candles. Dark pillows everywhere. The place was a wreck. He was older, with a Spanish-sounding accent, and I don't remember his name. But he had a sling, and my body was strung up and my legs were spread, and he punched my hole fast and hard, until I told him I could take more. He already knew I could take more. He greased up his hands and started sliding his second one in. I don't remember much about him or his body, but I remember his breath, how he held it, how he was transfixed on me. I was an altar to him.

He was not ugly, but he was not especially attractive. We didn't need to say that I was the best hole he would get for some time. And to my surprise, he was an incredible fisting top.

I'm gonna stretch you out ...

That was in the summer, before it got cold in the city. In the fall, I visited my family because I needed to get out of New York. My therapist encouraged this trip, despite the health warnings and risks, because she was a harm reduction counselor and said there was a mental health argument for getting out. The city was facing a likely winter lockdown and she knew that even though I had enjoyed a long sober streak, a dark and lonely winter indoors would be hard.

I flew down, had dinner with Mom and Dad and Jo, and flew back. On the train home from the airport, I got a text from my friend Jean-Michel, a beautiful Afro-Caribbean man with brown, all-knowing eyes and a curly dark beard. He told me he was free that night because his husband was out. I said I'd *come over*.

When I got to his apartment, I sensed his deep sadness. I held his body on mine and his eyes dipped. I asked what was wrong. He said things *weren't going well*.

"Winter," he said. "It's getting hard."

He produced small lines of ketamine on a little plate. While he separated them finely with a subway access card, I washed his dishes. He was alone, the place was a mess, and he needed someone to be a mother for a moment.

Holding the K, he led me into the playroom. "How good is it?" I asked. "I don't want to do too much."

"It's good."

I did too much.

Seconds after I stepped in the shower to clean my butthole, I started spiraling. I somehow managed to get one squirt of water in me and released it before I could no longer stand. That one squirt was miraculously enough. I was hungry because my body was naturally clean and ready for it. He held me on the floor of the shower as I quivered and lurched into him. He seemed both large and small, time stopped, my vision twisted around his body, and I was in a K-hole. My limbs stretched out into some sort of slimy goo, a kaleidoscope of shapes, with thought upon thought layered on top of each other, logs building a cabin surrounded by stars.

I was high.

I was aware that I was high and also questioning the nature of being high, its virtues and challenges. As I privately debated the value of my high, I also distrusted my ability to engage in this debate while being high. But how could anyone appreciate the moment of being high without being high?

I was high.

I was spinning out of control and somehow crawled across the bathroom floor into the playroom, onto the little bed where he put down towels and was mixing the lube. I pulled my legs back like a baby and grabbed my ankles and he said, "There you go baby, I'm gonna stretch you out."

I said, "I love you," and asked him to *please go slow*. And he said, "I love you too."

As he moved into me, finger by finger, the meaty part of his knuckles pushed against my hole, he guided me out of the dark cave of K and into the warm orange light above his shoulder. It was the truest kind of love, the one that only exists between fisters: complete trust. I was distinctly aware that I was not fucked up on a speedy drug like meth but on a slower, softer drug and this, I realized, was a form of harm reduction because I would not go all night or be too wild or reckless on this one. I was more aware of my limits and I was familiar with this gentle man because we had played before. I made a mental note to tell my therapist about this.

I felt incredibly proud. And incredibly high. We were, at once, made and unmade, we were strong and defenseless. That's what getting fisted feels like.

He listened to my words, fed me more. Then he pushed his full hand in, and I felt the suction pull him in me and then that was all of it. "Breathe," he said.

Breathe.

"I just want to adjust to it," I said. "Stay there."

"You're beautiful," he said. "Beautiful. I'm not going anywhere." He stayed. I relaxed. And he was fisting me. I told him to *call it a pussy*, to treat me like a girl, and he started that dirty cunt talk that makes me gasp and moan.

You want my fist in your pussy? Yes, oh yes, please. *You want me to stretch your pussy?* Yes, yes. Please. *Baby, I'm stretching your pussy.*

Fuck yes.

He got nastier with his words, derision dripping from his mouth like honey spit: *your big stretched pussy, your big sloppy faggot pussy, your fucking faggot pussy.*

He was fucking me with his arm.

As I came out of my watery high, every two-inch thrust along his wrist pulled me back to the surface of my body. "Wait," I said. "Wait, I'm coming out of it. I might need another bump."

"You don't need another bump," he said. "Tell me a story."

"What?"

"Tell me about the rope tied around your ankle."

"Oh. Okay. I grew up on a farm."

"Okay."

"Have you ever opened a bag of horse feed?"

He laughed at me. "I'm from the Bronx."

"When you pull the bag open, you pull on this string."

Fuck, baby, that feels so good!

"Keep going. You pull on the string."

"You pull on the string. The last time I was on my parent's farm, I opened some bags of horse feed."

Fuck!

"You want my punches?"

"Yes."

He started punching me. All the way out, then back in, faster. I could feel my pussy getting puffy and gaped, swelling at its edges.

"Keep going," he said. "You were feeding the horses."

"Yeah. I took the strings and wove them together — I think you call it a plait?"

"Plait. Yeah. That's what Black girls call it."

"I made this long, woven string with it and looped it four times around my ankle and tied it off. I can't take it off."

Alexander Cheves

Fuck, baby, punch fist me. Destroy my pussy.

"I'm fisting you. My cowboy. Birthing you like a cow. You like that?"

And on and on. We were in it.

I retreated back into that subverbal corridor of the mind, the holy place where I was there and not there, every motion taking me to the edge of orgasm, pulling me in and out of it, testing my threshold, building me up, dropping me back.

We were bizarre creatures. Guys like us would never know how the other side made love or what their rituals were. We had to stay on this side where we were safe. This was our place.

He bent over, keeping his hand in me, and kissed me. I pulled my ankles up to his shoulders, stared into his sad brown eyes, and let him take me to the barn, the animal of my body. I was bucking and braying in pleasure. He held the reins, and he fed me.

+ + +

Some practitioners might not want to admit this, but fisting has always been a drug-adjacent — if not drug-dependent — fetish. Its rise in gay male culture can be traced to the advent of synthetic drugs becoming widely available in American culture. It made its gay debut in the 70s in gay sex clubs in San Francisco and New York.

But the erotic practice of inserting a hand into a rectum or vagina has likely been around for thousands of years. We have Egyptian artifacts showing it. And some believe Michaelangelo's *The Last Judgment* in the Sistine Chapel also depicts fisting. It is a natural extension of our most common gestures and motions (rubbing, fingering, teasing), but the modern fisting scene is more than just sliding a hand into an orifice — and very hard play usually requires some chemicals. We get medicated to dance, to fuck, to be filled up.

Maybe that'll make a man out of you.
I got to go where the people dance.
I want some action, I want to live ...
I love the nightlife ...

Fisting is not strictly safe. It's a high-risk sex sport that requires years of training, regular practice, gradual stretching, communication, and patience.

And I love it. It is my favorite thing to do.

I was first fisted sober, then quickly found the chemical assistance that made it much easier. Jean-Michel didn't do anything extraordinary — he simply was a good top who knew how to control my focus, make my mind work. Making me tell him a story was brilliant because it worked as a kind of meditation, bringing fisting into my broader life, made it real, less scary. My body relaxed around the field and pastures of the farm. I was allowed to do this.

Although our night of punching was not as intense as the doubles, I regretted nothing about it. I felt safe from start to finish. I left his place feeling stronger and more capable. That's what great sex is supposed to feel like for everyone.

I focused my grip on his hand, relaxed it, played with it. These were my muscles, that was my tunnel. Like all my great lovers, I don't text him, don't call him. When we meet we promise, every time, to do so again soon, even though we won't. I've gone through the same pantomime and the same promises with everyone that I've shared that kind of connection with. I don't know what they see in me, but I must be a frustrating person to want.

Jean-Michel made me cum. We were slippery, trembling, my white body holding his brown body, my larger frame holding his smaller frame, my lips on his lips. I was connected to this beautiful, honest man. We made love, then rested on the bed. I asked him why he was so sad. It had to do with his husband.

"He has really bad depression." Jean-Michel smiled as he talked, and his smile betrayed some brokenness. "He got a new therapist and some new meds and now he's coming out of it and he asked me why I'm so distant. And I told him that he hasn't been here for months. He's not been in this relationship."

"Depression is hard," I said. "I struggle with it too."

"We all do," he said.

"Are you guys talking to anyone?"

"Yeah, we have a couples' therapist too."

"Everyone needs a therapist."

The ceiling above us had exposed rafters, odd in New York City, and I thought about how we all really struggled with depression. We both knew guys whose nerves were fried and had to leave the city or who had to go to rehab or were simply never seen again. We were, so many of us, children of some revolution that happened before us. We were its echo, its byproduct, its afterbirth. We would never be content except in cities and on dance floors. Visits to a family farm, memories of feeding horses, had their place and role. But we had to go find our own place, our own home for wayward boys, and we belonged in urban settings like New York, Amsterdam, Berlin, places where we could live and suffer and occasionally feel connected like this.

I thought, *Someday, he and I will be older people — old queens — if we survive being young. And we'll tell our therapists all about it.*

Someday. Right now, though,

I've got to boogie, on the disco 'round ...

Atonement

1. There is a beautiful man of color in Atlanta who, to date, has the biggest dick I've ever taken. When I lived there, I should have called him more, befriended him, seen him more than as just a great lay, a great slab of meat, because he seemed sincerely kind.

Unlike most very hung men, he actually knew how to fuck hole — how to give it pleasure, how to maximize the stretch of his size. He struggled to find bottoms who could take it. I was one of only two men he saw regularly, and bizarrely, the other guy — I never met him — was Deaf, and I was only halfway in the world of sound.

Sir, if you are reading this, I'd like you to know that you are the only man who has ever made me cum without touching myself, twice in a row.

Do you remember? It was dawn. The flowers bloomed outside your door and I bloomed in your bedroom. Wherever you are now, I hope you're doing okay.

2. To the man in San Francisco who fisted me for the first time: bless you. You awakened the beast in me when you opened me.

3. Many thanks to the man I met at Folsom some years ago: You are my best fisting session. You probably don't remember me. After that night, I asked other people in San Francisco about you, chased the memory of you around the city, passed your name through my friends, and those who knew you better spoke mostly of your kindness and goodness.

We passed each other on the stairs — I was going down, you were coming up — at a large fisting party. You said you liked my butt and wanted to play in it. I was very tired from the long night and was on my way to the door to leave, but you were handsome and tall and made me stop, stay. We cruised each other at the same moment, our heads turning as if they were coordinated around this little dance, peacocking, preening, animals in nature — fluffing our feathers, waving our horns.

When we realized we were linked, like dogs before pouncing, I felt your large hands and nearly laughed. "Sorry," I said. "I'm not that skilled."

You assured me I didn't have to be.

"No expectations," you said. "I just want to play in your butt." And I believed you — you were comforting, easing. And besides, it was the end of a good night, so whatever happened next was extra. A cherry on top.

We walked back up to the second floor — a large room with red lights in the ceiling and black sex slings lining the walls. Most of the slings were occupied by other people getting fisted, other members of our fraternity. We found an open one in the corner.

You started gently and seemed to know what you were doing. I really can't describe how it felt when you finally pushed in, but you took me to that other place, the one I dream about on my hungriest nights. A small crowd gathered around us and I heard muffled voices, the low sounds of priests watching over a ritual: *Oh yeah* and *Fuck yeah* and *That's beautiful.* Their voices were hollow, like echoes. I fell into the pit of myself, surrendered. A friend watched us and later told me that my legs were pulled so far back, my feet were nearly behind my head, my fist hole so presented, so spread. *Wreck me.*

I don't remember your details so much as I remember your dimensions, and how you said, *It's okay, lean back, I got you* — and I just let go. You pushed your hand in me, pulled it out, over and over. How long did it last? An hour? More? I think of that encounter when I weigh my life's bizarre highs and lows. You were one of the peaks. Thank you.

4. I've met many fabulous Queers with so many fascinating kinks, and I only want to meet more of them. They are the most amazing people. They are the sex radicals and faeries and rubber dogs and nonbinary Marxists and sex therapists and sex workers dotted through my life, notes on a map, connections I've tried — and often failed — to appreciate.

I'm not one to be delivering blessings, but if I could bless every person who taught me something I needed to know, loved me briefly, or both, I would send them out, command them like flying monkeys, make them go skittering across the waters.

5. To the anonymous saint I met in a sex club years ago: You were just a face, blue eyes — I think — with a short brown beard. I can guess your age, mid-forties maybe, but can't say for sure. It was dark. I don't know your name, of course.

This was some time in the year after my HIV diagnosis. I was on medication, but I still felt ugly and untouchable, something to be feared and unwanted. I nervously told you about my HIV and you said, "I don't give a shit about your status." Then you pushed me over and raped my ridiculous cunt like it was a toy you found in the gutter.

It was a small act of love, but it showed me that there were people like you — people like us — who really didn't care, who didn't need the long business of full disclosure. You were, in effect, my first glimpse into bareback culture in which sex pigs assume the risks and enjoy the rewards with pure, shared abandon. Men like us come together, skin against skin, bone on bone, to delight in common cum, common blame. Wherever — whoever — you are, thanks for bringing me into the fold and raising me from the dead.

6. I really cannot thank — or even list — all the gay guides, the mentors and daddies. There are too many. They gave me spare bedrooms and sofas to sleep on when I had nowhere, taught me about my history, sat down with me and said I needed to be better — with people, with money, with myself.

What would they think of this list of atonement — this lineup of people I should have loved? Is this being better? Do they approve?

7. Some faggots I have known said the words *I love you* after just one brief conversation. When they did this, it frightened me. I never tell anyone that, and when I do, I never say all three words or give the phrase its complete weight. I make it simpler and smaller. When I say it to my parents, I condense it to *love you*, something quick, a customary flick of the tongue before hanging up the phone. I say it to my boyfriend in a cute, bumbling voice so that it becomes a soft thing, nothing with edges or teeth, nothing to hold on to. I struggle with *I love you* in its fullness, but others do not, and they taught me that love is reckless and does not demand anything back.

8. For a bartender in a city I used to live in: I've kept a little flame for you. At this point, my crush is something of a joke. Ber teases me about it. The first time you caught my eye, you were making someone else's drink and I saw your impressive tattoo, an eagle with its wings spread across your back, its wingtips curling over your shoulders. I know that admitting something like this is ridiculous, but I am a ridiculous person. Everyone falls for the bartender at some point.

Do you remember the first time we fucked? We were on a dance floor in a club that has been torn down and replaced with luxury apartments. I think we were both high on MDMA. I was still new to the city and you recognized me from the bar. More than new, I was green — fresh from L.A., knowing nothing, trying to impress everyone. I was pushy. I was annoying.

I danced and rubbed against you. You were at least a foot taller than me, and you danced over me, then pulled my hand to your black shorts and I felt your cock and was surprised at how big it was. I squeezed it and slid my hand in your pants. Then you grabbed me by the wrist and pulled me off the dance floor. I thought you were angry at me for touching you and wondered if we had miscommunicated desire. I've read signals wrong before, especially on dance floors.

But you pulled me through a room, two, then to the bathroom, locked the door behind us, pulled down my pants, and told me to bend over the toilet. All we had was your spit for lube and I struggled because you were so tall and because it really hurt, and I hate getting fucked in that stupid standing position. I couldn't relax and was disappointed in my performance because I really wanted you.

Our first time wasn't great, but it was the first of a few. You said you had a thing for holes filled with other men's cum. One night at the bathhouse, I begged you to come over and you said you would only come after I was filled with *as many guys as possible*. So, after a few hours — after I was actually leaking sperm while walking through the halls — you came, found me in the sling, my legs already in the stirrups, and sent me home sore.

Now we live in different cities, and although I've run into you once or twice — people like us pass through the same places on loop, over and over, bound to collide — the newness of those early hookups has long since worn off. I'm someone you know and you're someone I know. We never connected outside of sex and we never needed to. But I was impressed when, after COVID-19 hit, you started making masks for medical workers and shipping them out by the hundreds for free every week. I thought that was kind and generous, and those honorable traits so often go unrewarded among people like us.

The older I get, the more I value and understand those core virtues — *kindness, generosity* — which we were taught to appreciate as children. But as children, those words have only a vague meaning. As a child, sharing means sharing toys, not cum. It's strange that the simplest words became more mysterious and complicated — *grace, love* — and revealed themselves in the thrill and fury of fucking. You were a sex pig, but I've met many sex pigs. Not all of them were good people. Or good bartenders.

9. In a city I used to live in is a doctor who saw a young man that needed a sober friend. I wonder sometimes if he avoids talking to me now because I have issues with 12-step programs, which I tend to air too vocally. When I think about him, I am reminded that my animosity against the program must be checked — that a person can prefer one approach to wellness without despising the others. He is one of those guides I am thankful for, and he was saved by the program, so I must bless the program too, because it brought him into my life to save me.

My friend: your existence is as a lighthouse. You know this. You are evidence to me and others that life can happen on the other side of dark places. If I ever fall too hard and need the ritual of the rooms and the mandate of sobriety to come back, I know you will be there, welcoming me as if I never left.

10. I met a girl in my junior year of college. She was much taller than me. She had blonde hair and green eyes. We went to the coffee shop on Bull Street and talked about books we loved. I loved *Lolita*; she hated it. She loved *The Great Gatsby* and I've never been able to finish it. We both loved *One Hundred Years of Solitude* and disagreed on Sartre and thought short stories by Borges were important, if not especially enjoyable.

If you're reading this: Please know that, in those talks, I fell in love with you, but I didn't know how to communicate that because I didn't know love was allowed.

I thought I could only be gay. The idea of reappraising that word felt like a betrayal of self. You are one of the most beautiful people I've ever met. You were unwilling to be soft or gentle in the world and often told me that, as a woman and artist, you had to be willing and ready to abandon anyone at any moment in order to climb. I envied your fury. Later, I emulated it. I wanted to be like you.

One day we were standing by my truck. We spent the afternoon talking, and as the sun fell and we said goodbye, you said, "I don't know if you want to kiss me."

I was shocked and asked you what you meant.

"Nothing, I'm just being silly. I love you." You hugged me and walked away.

My untamable girl, I wish I had kissed you. I just didn't know how.

11. In my first year of college, I became close with two other freshmen: a man who then identified as straight and a woman, fiery and olive-skinned, and we spent almost every minute together.

Except at night. At night, he would lie down next to me and pull my shirt off. I laid on my stomach and he gently ran his fingers over my back, just touching the soft hair of my skin, and made me guess the patterns. There were figure 8s, words, messages, confessions. I remember his loops and spirals down my body, long and slow, dropping lower and lower until his fingertips plucked over my hole.

He knew what he was doing and always held back, working me up until I was hungry, angry, and pulled him on top of me. The sex was sloppy, and I don't think he particularly enjoyed it.

I didn't know that the careful touching was the true sex. I could not appreciate it as sex then. Sex lived in a narrow box, required some degree of penetration. Taking someone in me or being inside someone else was, I thought, for me and for all, the ultimate desire. I had no idea what touching could be, how much more powerful it could be than breeding.

These little discoveries ended the day the three of us climbed in the shower together. I don't know why we did this. We were still in our clothes. At first it was funny, sitting there, getting wet.

But then we looked at each other. Her eyes were dark brown, wolf-like, and I wanted to touch her, and I wanted him to touch me. We were not tender; we were just looking. We talked, shoulder to shoulder. We were children and didn't know what this was or what it could be. We didn't have the language — we didn't know what threesomes were.

Then my old demon slipped out and I realized I was just in the way. They wanted each other and I was just there. I stood up without a word and stepped out. I heard them calling for me. I dried off my clothes as much as I could with a towel and walked out the door.

12. An ocean away, on a hilltop in Zambia, I sat with an orphan named Jacob, talking.

He was close to my age, and he was handsome. He had big, excited eyes and beautiful Black skin, strong features, a natural playfulness. I was visiting the orphanage with a missionary team, years before I came out, and I connected with Jacob — we played soccer in the field and drew things in the sand.

We went to the hilltop. I was afraid of snakes, but he was not.

If you write about a snake, it's a dick. It's always going to be a dick. We sat on the rocks overlooking the valley and spoke more openly — about his life, the violence he had experienced, how he walked on foot to the nearest city, Livingstone, dug around in the trash for food, and someone found him and brought him to the orphanage.

And then I noticed it, that little fire, the light in his eyes. It was the mark of kinship. He was like me.

I can't be certain of this, of course, but I think he was trying to flirt with me without having a language in which to do it or even a concept, a reality, in which that was permissible. The orphanage was run by Christians. I knew what I was, the word *gay* was hidden in me like a bomb, but I was new to it, and sharing it would be dangerous. It would reveal me and, if he wasn't careful, if he didn't understand what the word was, what adults often did with it, it would reveal him too, and in this country, that could forfeit his life.

He was a troublemaker at the little school on the compound. The house mothers scolded him, and the visiting teams loved him. He was bright and warm and I'm sure there was some fear that he would have sex with one of the girls at the orphanage. I didn't think that would happen.

I sensed it; the thing known between animals of the same order. We talked about what subjects he liked in school, we laughed, and then it ended. We held hands on the path back to the compound, but that meant nothing — or everything — in Africa because heterosexual men often held hands. This was a socially acceptable form of affection in a country that might murder someone for sodomy.

I did not give him the words. I thought I was refraining for his safety, but truly I just refrained for mine.

He might have been horrified at my message of a different god. He might have run off to tell an adult. I was still in the closet and Mom and Dad were on the missionary team with me.

Should I have said something? Could I have? The only thing I could have given him was the word. *Gay*. I could not have kissed him or held him or done anything else.

If you're reading this, my brother, know that no one else can save you. If you want to be free — truly free — you have to do it. You have to claw your way out. You must be willing and ready to burn down everything in your life in order to live.

Prayer

When you moved across the waters, when did you first see us crawling out of the earth? Did you see us in the beginning of our story, committing our first sins, or at its end?

I really don't know how godhood works, but I would like to. I've lost friends to COVID-19 and a generation of men before me lost many of their friends to AIDS, so I suppose I'd like some clarity, some glimpse of your design. Your apologists, when presented with your cruelty, defend you. They say: *We cannot know the mind of god.*

Can we not? I tested positive for HIV at 21. Was that really necessary? Someone takes blood out of my arm every few months to make sure the medications are still working. I don't mean to sound ungrateful, but that needle hurts every time, and I have to put my hand over my eyes because I can't bear the sight of my own blood outside my body.

I speak as if you were listening. It's nice to pretend.

I don't actually believe in you, but my parents do, so there was a time when I believed in you, too. That's how faith works. One hangover from it is that I've never been able to stop the regular impulse to pray. You are like a bad habit, a burn at the roof of my mouth I keep tonguing. This habit lets me focus my anger, sharpen it, direct it at something. Prayers of rage occasionally slip out.

Where were you when I laid the foundations of the Earth?

Would you like to know more about me? I live in New York City. I suppose you know that. It seems silly to speak to you this way, but I guess the time for pretenses between us is over. We can truly speak honestly with each other.

Alexander Cheves 205

And speaking honestly, let me just say that I have fallen in love with too many people in my life and I would very much like not to lose any of them, if it suits you. And for what it's worth, I like living. Maybe I should say *thank you*. Some people would tell me to get down on my knees and beseech you to keep me here, tethered to this world. I don't want to die, but I don't kneel for anything but dick.

Humans have to end someday, and our best scientists say our extinction will likely come with some horrible, uncontrollable disease. Not COVID-19. Something worse. I wonder what you have in mind.

Or are we just being uncreative? Will the sun explode? Will a comet come crashing in or, more thrillingly, will some extraterrestrial being come and wipe us out? On your timeline, we must look like blips of static. And yet some say you know every hair on our heads. I don't know why anyone worships you or anything like you. You're just too big, too monstrous.

Still, I pretend that you listen. And not just now. I pray all the time!

If you've been listening, you know how scared I am. I have HIV — another one of your cruel and careless larks — and right now, no one seems to know if HIV will worsen my chances of surviving COVID-19 in the years ahead. It would be comically awful of you to give me both.

I must ask: Do we look any different to you from the people in the Middle Ages who begged for healing while their bodies turned black and boiled? What about people in Africa with AIDS and malaria, dying over the last 40 years, lifting their arms in prayer? You may not have seen them, but I have. I lived there. They dragged themselves across the bush to be prayed for. They clung to hope. I prayed with them and watched them die. If not them, to whom do you listen?

I have many feelings about my life, which are worth examining now that the world seems so very fucked. For the record, I think I'm okay. I'm decently capable and more than decently loved. I have been given enough. I am a bratty recipient of privilege.

Is this some kind of concession? Is this a truce? I will not hate you any less for these gifts, but I also don't want to be an old man punching ghosts in the wind. So, why don't we call it even?

You know what I am capable of. I have done some amazing and disgusting things with my body, and I am comparatively tame next to others I've known. I hope you watched every detail, marked every thrust, and witnessed me become something that thrives in a world without you.

It may not be my place to make this offer, but if the burden of godhood is too heavy or the view too boring and you'd like to be relieved for a minute, let me sit where you sit. Let me bear the crown for a day.

I don't know what I'd do if you granted me this, your vision, your wisdom. If I could see the sum of all toil in one glance, would I weep? Would I weigh the horror and genocide and slavery, smiting everyone for what they've done? I decided some years ago when I tested positive that my life was worth living no matter what, and I still believe that. But I don't know if I could make that choice for everyone. I could not say for every sufferer out there that life holds more joy than pain.

I would simply do what you have not done. I would bend down and embrace everyone, give the world lasting evidence that someone's listening, that someone cares. I would show them mercy and love. And I would whisper in everyone's ear on your behalf:

Please, please forgive me.

As a child, I was told your love was benevolent, something that moved mountains and parted oceans. With the Biblical study of a good son, I learned your love was also jealous and wrathful. And with some life behind me, I learned it could not be love at all, unless love at the cosmic scale translates to negligence, to absence. Whatever it is, I respect that it's very, very big, very impressive — a vast void of *could have been,* and my love is nothing like that.

My love is a beast, not a big one, but alive and real. The beast may be faulty, lame, limited by time and ability — all unknown to you. My love is from the wild, carnal. My love is *fucking.* My love is present, hands-on, hands-in. Like your love, mine can make some people rapt with joy and others beg in their suffering. It goes where I go, dies when I die. And when it does — when I take my last suck of air and my love goes dark — it will be on your directive. You decide when all my love stories end. Until then, I will consider us competitors, if not foes, and I will fight you for the hearts of men.

Virus

The End Times seem like any other day. I'm looking out my window at South Brooklyn, from my balcony on the 28th floor of my apartment building. The reds and browns of Bay Ridge are broken only by black steeples and dark green patches of the park. Nothing is amiss. The Verrazzano-Narrows stretches to Staten Island in the fog. No four horsemen yet.

I'm looking south, down the eastern spine of America. My parents — two doctors — hear alarming reports from nurses who've traveled to New York to help our sick and dying. They want me to return to the farm. I haven't given them an answer yet. They believe my chances of getting a ventilator, should I get very sick, are better down South than here.

A pandemic is, among other things, awful writer's block. This isn't helped by everyone saying, *At least you have plenty of time to write now!*

For the love of god, shut up.

No one writes when it's convenient to. In fact, I don't know any writers who actually like sitting down to do it. Writing cuts itself into your life like a ghost that only comes out after you already made dinner plans, or late at night when you should be sleeping. My best bursts come between 9:30 pm and midnight, after I leave the gym.

My walks from the gym to the train are my greatest happiness. I'm sore, sweaty, raw, elated. I go up the steps from the gym and onto 42nd Street. The top of the stairs always smells like cigarette smoke. The building has been covered in scaffolding since I moved here, and people go there to smoke and stay out of the weather.

The entrance is on a sketchy block, at least as far as gentrified Manhattan goes. I've seen everything from the entrance: drug hand-offs, people pissing and shitting in broad daylight, overdosed people on the ground surrounded by paramedics, countless people crouching around, growling obscenities at everyone, fights, and almost-fights. I leave the entrance, turn left, walk past the convenience store playing Vivaldi on an outdoor speaker, past the Holy Cross Church, past the Greek Trattoria, past the Army surplus store.

Ahead, shining in terrible glory, is Times Square. This isn't Times Square proper — the meat of it is just around the corner. This is just the edges, the borderland where the city surrenders to ad space, where the crowds start to gather. I skirt most of it, but as I step into the train station, I can look left down 7th Avenue at the multitude, a sea of people choked together between walls of video ads rising into the sky like electric teeth.

I pass Five Guys Burgers and Madame Tussaud's across the street. Past the Lyric Theater, home to *Harry Potter and the Cursed Child*. Everywhere I look are tourists. I have to step around them. They're planted, mouths agape in joy and horror, transfixed by the splendor of Applebee's and M&Ms.

In that dizzying corridor, celebrity faces smile down at us. They are benevolent. They sell shoes or toothbrushes or pet food. In the station, someone plays the saxophone. A child, not a day over ten, sings catchy pop anthems into a microphone. I go deeper — the Times Square station is monstrous, a labyrinth of corridors and stairways where millions of people cough and sneeze on each other every day — and wait for the train to Brooklyn. If I'm lucky, the girl I love to hear is playing her violin, achingly, breaking the noise of people with songs of mourning. I always want to tip her, but she plays on the uptown platform.

This three-block walk makes me write. I go home, make tea, sit at my computer, and put something down. If I have anything to say, this is when it happens. Losing this ritual has been hard. I would give anything to get on a train, just to pretend I was coming home from the gym, but public transit is out of the question.

In New York City, I can get anywhere by train. The trains take me to more trains or to the airport. It's alarming how effortlessly I can travel from Pretoria to the Bronx. New Yorkers are ruing this lost accessibility as we shelter in place in the red-hot epicenter of COVID-19. This city currently has more cases and hospitalizations than any place on earth. I don't know today's numbers, but more people are dying every hour. On news stations, New York City is a big red dot on the map of America. Our dot is so big and bright that it expands over our neighbors and nearby states like a bomb, outshining the country. It looks like something from a horror movie, but it's real.

I thought the world would be more prepared for something like this. Here at the end, there are still billionaires, and they're doing fine, from what I hear. But the Japanese bakery near my train stop has disappeared for good. Before the pandemic, the kind lady there sold warm egg buns in the morning for $1.50. She always said hi to me, like she was happy to see me. And now her shop is gone. I have no words for it all, so here are some from Wordsworth:

The world is too much with us; late and soon,
Getting and spending, we lay waste our powers

A confession: Some time ago, I stopped exploring sexually with the passion and curiosity I once had. I lost some moxie. I've been in a lengthy dry spell, one that's not likely to end with the pandemic, and it has made me doubt everything — my work, my attractiveness, my value among gay men, even my identity as a happy slut.

Kink, in its way, saved me. My kinks stay hidden in my body, like my sluthood, alive even in hibernation. When I walk through the empty city, my kinks are hidden in plain sight. They are me, the shadowed me. My sexual identity is not contingent upon sex. I'm still real. I'm just a person — an adult now, I think — and I can have doubts. I am allowed to feel numb.

Sluts don't get made just in big cities or at sex parties. We crawl out of small towns, country farms, mountain passes. My stories are mostly written from experiences in cities, but I long ago rejected the idea that cities are the only epicenters of hedonism — they are, if anything, just places where more people are willing to buy sex. I have stayed in cities for the work, but as someone from the woods, I've never fully adjusted to them.

I'm mildly more mature now and wiser than I was in San Francisco and L.A. — and a bit quieter, a little better with money, somewhat more willing to linger. Ber has always known what I am. The bad spirit in me still wants to leave. Sometimes, Ber finds me sitting on the sofa, staring at the wall or looking out the window, and he knows I'm dreaming of the next place.

Amsterdam. Berlin. London.

But I'm still here, and if I have a home now, I guess it's with him. We can call it love. It's very frightening. This must be what staying feels like.

+ + +

Even with the pandemic, I'm happy to be in this city. If I follow my parents' orders and return to the farm, I wonder if this will be the moment when I say everything, when I tell Dad how much I love him and that I understand him, that I forgive him and need him to forgive me.

Will I tell Mom that I don't want any other mom? Someday I must tell her that the mystery of that woman, whoever she was, who gave birth to me is no longer a story that interests me. I don't need a dancer. I need Mom.

Will I tell my sister, Jo, how cool she is?

Mass deaths are a good time to make amends.

When I need to be outside, I run to the bridge. The closer I get to it, the more in awe I become. It's just so big. The Verrazzano-Narrows is the longest cable suspension bridge in the Western hemisphere. But what really fascinates me are all the streets and neighborhoods of Bay Ridge between my building and the bridge. On every block, there's a bakery or a church, a place worth seeing, and in all the windows, lives worth fantasizing about. When I moved here, I grumbled about leaving Manhattan, which now seems childish. Everything I need is anywhere I am.

Here are some words by Matthew Dickman, which remind me what's at stake in this age of separation:

This is the almond grove
in the dark slow dance.
It is what we should be doing right now. Scraping
for joy.

As I write this, night is falling over Brooklyn. The bridge is beautiful — the lights on its cables are just twinkling on in the blue dusk. It would be dangerous to be here with me, but I wish everyone could see it.

Acknowledgements

This book, and my ability to write it, would not exist without the many teachers and friends who have guided, critiqued, and supported me. I thank my professors at the Savannah College of Art and Design, especially Jonathan Rabb and Angela Brandt. I am indebted to the generous editors, writers, and staff at *The Advocate* for taking a chance on an intern — in particular, Sunnivie Brydum, Neal Broverman, Christopher Harrity, Daniel Reynolds, Lucas Grindley, Tracy E. Gilchrist, and Diane Anderson-Minshall. I am also grateful for Mikelle Street at *Out Magazine*, as well as my editors at *Them, VICE, TheBody,* and all the other publications I've had the privilege to write for. My thanks to Tyler Trykowski, Mathew Rodriguez, David Artavia, Nico Lang, and many others who made my writing better. To Amariah Love: this book was made better by your sensitive, careful reading and critically important thoughts. Stephan Ferris provided essential legal counsel, for which I am thankful.

I thank Mark Hill, Joe and Matty, Neon, cousin Mallory, and everyone who let me crash in their spare rooms and on their sofas. I am deeply appreciative of Stephen Pevner, who gave me a beautiful place to write during the COVID-19 lockdown and access to vital New York City gay history documents. I thank the readers of my blog, *Love, Beastly*, especially those who have kindly donated to my Patreon in support of my work.

Every writer surely wants a creative partnership like the one I have with Patrick Davis, the publisher at Unbound Edition Press. Thank you, my friend, for the unyielding faith and endless encouragement.

I thank my boyfriends and lovers for the stories. I thank my boyfriend Brent for putting up with me. I thank Mom, Dad, and my sister Rebecca for loving me through my best and most challenging moments alike.

And lastly, I thank the ones I will never know — those who fought a plague and liberated me and all future faggots by refusing to simply die. Strangers — on dance floors, in dark places — are perhaps most responsible for my life, including the most enigmatic one: a woman I will likely never meet, who decided, perhaps at the last minute, that I should live.

Notes and Sources

This work contains excerpts and references to specific works by other authors and such uses are made and intended as Fair Use of each such work under the United States copyright laws. The author and publisher provide the applicable attribution to these works based on readily available public information.

The chapter "Ghosts" contains lines from Jack Kerouac's "Heaven" in *Heaven & Other Poems*. Copyright © 1959, 1960, 1977 by Estate of Jack Kerouac. Published by Grey Fox, an imprint of City Lights Books.

The chapter "Tongue" contains lines from Nicki Minaj's "Roman's Revenge." Lyrics copyright © 2011 by Onika Maraj. Published by Universal Music Publishing.

The chapter "Guide" contains the poem "The Love Song of an All-American Hero." Copyright © 2013 by Alex W. Cheves. Published by the Savannah College of Art and Design in *Artemis*.

The chapter "Xmas" contains lines from Vladimir Nabokov's *Lolita*. Copyright © 1955 by Vladimir Nabokov. Published by Vintage Books, a division of Penguin Random House.

The chapter "Faithless" contains Epicurus's trilemma, summarized by Hume and others, and known commonly as "the problem of evil."

The chapter "Hotel" contains lines from C.K. Williams's "The Gas Station" in *Collected Poems*. Copyright © 2006 by C.K. Williams. Published by Farrar, Strauss and Giroux, a division of Macmillan.

The chapter "Bathhouse" contains lines from Tina Turner's "What's Love Got to Do With It." Written by Terry Britten and Graham Lyle. Lyrics copyright © 1984 by WB Music Corp.

The chapter "June" contains lines from Mark Strand's "Eating Poetry" in *Selected Poems*. Copyright © 1980 by Mark Strand. Published by Alfred A. Knopf, a division of Penguin Random House.

The chapter "Doubles" contains lines from Alicia Bridges's "I Love the Nightlife (Disco 'Round)." Lyrics copyright © 1978 by Alicia Bridges and Susan Hutcheson.

The chapter "Virus" contains lines from William Wordsworth's poem "The World Is Too Much With Us."

The chapter "Virus" contains lines from Matthew Dickman's "Slow Dance" in *All American Poem*. Copyright © 2008 by Matthew Dickman. Published by The American Poetry Review.

The author and publisher make no claim of any rights whatsoever to the works cited and excerpted for artistic and critical purposes in this book, with the singular exception of "The Love Song of an All-American Hero," which is the author's own work.

About the Type and Paper

Designed by Malou Verlomme of the Monotype Studio, Macklin is an elegant, high-contrast typeface. It has been designed purposely for more emotional appeal.

The concept for Macklin began with research on historical material from Britain and Europe dating to the beginning of the 19th century, specifically the work of Vincent Figgins. Verlomme pays respect to Figgins's work with Macklin, but pushes the family to a more contemporary place.

This book is printed on natural Rolland Enviro Book stock. The paper is 100 percent post-consumer sustainable fiber content and is FSC-certified.

Unbound Edition Press champions honest, original voices.
Committed to the power of writers who explore and illuminate
the contemporary human condition, we publish collections of poetry,
short fiction, and essays. Our publisher and editorial team aim to identify,
develop, and defend authors who create thoughtfully challenging work
which may not find a home with mainstream publishers.
Guided by a mission to respect and elevate emerging, overlooked,
or LGBTQ+ authors, we work to make meaningful contributions to
the literary arts by publishing their work.

unboundedition.com